Fichte and the Vocation of the Intellectual:
A Founding Figure of German Idealism

—A Founding Figure of German Idealism—

FICHTE

—and the Vocation of the Intellectual—

DIEGO FUSARO

Translated by
Anna Carnesecchi

ANTELOPE HILL PUBLISHING

Cover art by Swifty.
Edited by Victoria Smith.
Formatted by Margaret Bauer.

Antelope Hill Publishing
antelopehillpublishing.com

Paperback ISBN-13: 978-1-956887-38-9
EPUB ISBN-13: 978-1-953730-94-7

♦

He only is free, who would make all around him free likewise, and does really make them free.

J.G. Fichte, *The Vocation of the Scholar*

♦

Fichte is a titan who fights for humanity and whose circle of influence will definitely not remain within the walls of the auditorium.

F. Hölderlin

♦

About the Author

DIEGO FUSARO (1983) teaches History of Philosophy at
the IASSP (Institute for Higher Strategic and Political
Studies) in Milan. He is an attentive student of the
history of Marxism and of German and Italian idealism,
as well as a counter-current interpreter of the present.
He also collaborates with "Il Fatto Quotidiano" and
"Affari Italiani." Among his most successful books we
find: *Welcome Back Marx! Rebirth of a Revolutionary
Thought* (Bompiani 2009), *Thinking Otherwise* (Einaudi
2017), *The New Erotic Order* (Rizzoli 2018), and
Globalization (Rizzoli 2019).

Contents

♦

♦

Under what I call philosophy, there cannot be anything that is static, immobile, or dead. In philosophy, everything is action, movement, and life; philosophy does not find anything, but makes everything rise under her own eyes to such extent that I entirely refuse the name of philosophy, as if it were a business of dead concepts.

J.G. Fichte, *From a private letter,* January 1800
English translation by A. Carnesecchi.

♦

A man who isolates himself gives up to his destiny; he does not care about the moral progress. Speaking in moral terms, to think only of yourself is the same thing as not thinking of yourself at all, because the absolute end of the individual lies not inside him, but in humanity as a whole.

J.G. Fichte, *The System of Ethics*
English translation by A. Carnesecchi.

♦

1.

Genesis and History of the Work

♦

One can apply to Fichte, more than any other author who belongs to the Western canon, Foucault's thought on any thinker, indistinctively from their context and their specific theoretical standpoint. "The unique unity that we can acknowledge in an author's work," wrote the philosopher, "is a specific function of expression," a horizon of meaning that often is neither made explicit nor coherent, but that is the *basso continuo* of his lucubration.[1] In order to grasp it, one needs to start off the "long journey" of a "surplus labor of hermeneutics" beginning with the quotations of the thinker's work and showing in which sense they enclose in a concise form the expressive function of his thought. If it is true that the book

---

[1] Michel Foucault, *Sur l'archéologie des sciences. Réponse au Cercle d'épistémologie*, 1968; translated in Italian by A. Cutro, S*ull'archeologia delle scienze. Risposta al Circolo di epistemologia*, in Id., *Il sapere e la storia. Sull''archeologia delle scienze e altri scritti*, (Verona: Ombre Corte, 2007), p. 41. English translation by A. Carnesecchi.
[2] M. Foucault, *The Archaeology of Knowledge and the Discourse on Language*, trans. by A.M. Sheridan Smith, (New York: Pantheon Books, 1972), p. 23.

does not end with the pages that enclose (and apparently fulfill) the message, it is also true that in the nomadic pluralism of the texts (or, not rarely, of the very same text) comprising the prismatic constellation of the opus, it is necessary to retrace—beyond the fragmented proliferation of meaning and allusions—a structural unity, a unitary function, a common horizon which could allow one to understand and locate the thinker and his scattered fragments.

This *aporia* is, on the other hand, amplified if one considers while following Foucault's footprints, that not only the thought but also the single work tends inexorably to escape any attempt to rigorously trace the borders and limits, inasmuch as it is part of a constellation of texts and cross-references that cannot be expressed in the printed pages in which the work is apparently confined. As Foucault explains:

> *The frontiers of a book are never clear-cut: beyond the title, the first lines, and the last full stop, beyond its internal configuration and its autonomous form, it is caught up in a system of references to other books, others texts, other sentences: It is a node within a network.*

As implied, Fichte's can be employed as a paradigmatic case of the elusive and protean character of an author's opus. This is not only because of the multidimensional structure of a work in progress that is the *Wissenschaftslehre* (*The Doctrine of Knowledge*)—with its twelve versions handled in printed pages as well as in drafts of private manuscripts;[2] but also, and perhaps especially, because of his *The Vocation of the Scholar* (*Bestimmung des Gelehrten*). The latter, an authentic "node within a network," is not only a book resulting from a series of

---

[2] On the genesis and editorial history of the *Wissenschaftslehre* see the classical work by M. Guéroult *L'évolution et la structure de la Doctrine de la Science chez Fichte*, (Hildesheim: Olms, 1930-1982). See also J. Hyppolite, *L'idée de la doctrine de la science et le sens de son évolution chez Fichte*, in *Etudes sur l'histoire de la philosophie en homage a Martial Guéroult*, (Paris: Fischbacher, 1964), pp. 93-108.

public lectures given in Jena in 1794, but has both the unsettling form of a thick web of references to the culture of its time and to the debates that animated it, as well as the comprehensive theoretical elaboration of its author, his majestic *Wissenschaftslehre* upon which Fichte kept on working while giving other university lectures. Among these lectures, *The Vocation of the Scholar* is nothing but a coherent social and political fulfillment of it.

While further developing Foucault's hint, one would be tempted to assert that Fichte's overall production is like a heated melting pot of ideas, a rich and heterogeneous constellation of texts, lectures, manuscripts, drafts, and essays that orbit around the holistic and founding project of *Wissenschaftslehre* that—as an authentic system of philosophical truth—is able to demonstrate its real wholeness given by its dynamic unity together with its specific determinations.[3] *The Vocation of the Scholar* is just one (not, of course, the only one) of its possible realizations on the political and social level.[4] It is the meeting point between the theoretical principles of *Wissenschaftslehre* and the actual way mankind (and in this particular case, intellectuals) act in accordance with these principles in the social sphere, along the moving ground of history, and in the agonal network of society. It is only from this perspective that *The Vocation of the Scholar*, the text in which the ineludibly practical, social, and political vocation of Fichte's reflection shines through, can be thereon understood.[5] Hence, *The Vocation of the Scholar* is also the text

---

[3] On this point, and especially on the matter of the determinations of Fichte's system, see F. Ferraguto, *Filosofare prima della filosofia: il problema dell'introduzione alla dottrina della scienza di J. G. Fichte*, (Hildesheim: Olms, 2010).

[4] See the monographic study by G. G. Stelli, *La ricerca del fondamento: il programma filosofico dell'idealismo tedesco nello scritto di Fichte "Sul concetto della dottrina della scienza,"* (Milan: Guerini, 1995).

[5] This aspect has been effectively highlighted by Cesare Luporini in *Fichte e la destinazione del dotto*, in "Società," (1947), pp. 193-216. Luporini shows how, to some extent, the *Bestimmung des Gelehrten* is the most coherent sociopolitical development of the *Wissenschaftslehre*'s program.

upon which to focus in order to decipher the origin of Fichte's thought. *The Vocation of the Scholar's* genesis in 1794 and its editorial case are essential to understand the existing nexus (not at all easeful and unambiguous) that links the thinker to the actual events of his time and therefore, to the existing relation between his work and the sociopolitical context, which is too much a part of the inextricable net in which any book is placed.[6]

As is well known, *The Vocation of the Scholar* is the result of five public lectures given by Fichte at the University of Jena between May and June 1794. The *Catalogus praelectionum*, that is the official program of the learning activities of the university written in Latin, according to the use of the time, announced the series of public lectures meant as meetings open to everyone without exclusions, and therefore not only for philosophy students, as was the case for the lectures that Fichte was giving at the same time on *Wissenschaftslehre*. Furthermore, the official program that scheduled lectures for the summer semester presented a series of gatherings with the grandiose title *"De officiis eruditorum,"* which is literally "on the duties of the scholars" or "learned people." As will be demonstrated in the following pages of this work, this translation from Latin, irreproachable on literal grounds, is actually deeply ambiguous, if not misleading, on the conceptual one. By annihilating the social and political value of the original meaning of the word scholars (*Gelehrten*), and consequently by reducing the intellectual to a learned person as an end in itself, it winds up contradicting the spirit of Fichte's teaching. The risk is that for the word "scholar," solely a theorist is meant who lives in an "ivory tower" extremely far from that society from which, according to Fichte, he cannot be

---

[6] Hints towards this direction can be at least partially found in the monographic essay by C. Amadio, *Logica della relazione politica: uno studio su "La dottrina della scienza" (1794/5) di J.G. Fichte*, (Milan: Giuffrè, 1998). Amadio insists on several occasions on the, by no means secondary, links between the *Doctrine of Science* and its concrete social, political, and historical-philosophical determinations concerning Fichte's galaxy of other writings.

detached. If so, he may fall into corrupt forms of a solipsistic culture devoid of any relation with mankind's emancipation that is transcendentally conceived as a unitary subject. Besides—as it was observed since the beginning—it would be an utter paradox if these lectures, destined to a public not familiar with the topic, had then as their subject scholars as traditionally meant, viz. that this social class first of all was identified because of its separation from society and its direct and exclusive contact with knowledge, then conceived as elitist good, merely theoretical and devoid of any social or political implication.

Moreover, it cannot be ignored that originally the series of meetings called *"De officiis eruditorum"* were not meant to be published. If then Fichte decided to do so and spread his lectures out, it was due to reasons linked to the political events of his time and to the author's position characterized by a fruitful union of coherence, courage, and honesty, all features that would accompany Fichte for his entire life. In doing so, not only does Fichte exemplify the sociopolitical mission of the scholar, but he also showed the sociopolitical vocation of the *Wissenschaftslehre* and its theoretical pillar: The importance of social action in order to transform the existing actuality by adapting it to the principles of an active subjectivity, the so-called "pure I" (*Ich*), identified with a mankind transcendentally conceived.[7]

Why, therefore, did Fichte decide to publish his lectures? What did persuade him to do so, even if originally his work was conceived for a different purpose? In order to answer these questions, we need to look back at the events Fichte was involved in a year before he started his course in 1794, when the University of Jena—which is after Weimar the most

---

[7] On this point will be built the interpretation of Fichte's opus and in particular, of the *Vorlesungen* (lectures) on the scholar as realization of the third principle of the doctrine of science, which posits a conflict between empirical *Is* and empirical *not-I's* and thereon, the empirical *Is*' moral effort to change the world so that it is compliant with Reason.

relevant city in the Duchy of Saxony—was feverishly looking for a professor of the highest repute who would occupy the vacant chair of philosophy. The post had until then been occupied by Reinhold who, before spring 1794, would have left it vacant as he intended to work at the University of Kiel. Therefore, the University of Jena needed to find a substitute up to Reinhold's level in regard to his speculative rigor and reputation among a large audience.

All the attention immediately converged on Fichte. With his *Attempt at a Critique of All Revelation (Versuch einer Kritik aller Offenbarung,* 1792), Fichte had achieved an impressive fame, but also raised a lively and wide debate in which Kant himself had to intervene to clarify that the book, which initially appeared as anonymous, was not his, even though the lexicon and the argumentative structure employed could legitimately cast a doubt as to Kant's original authorship.[8] In particular, what especially had led one to think so was the attempt in Fichte's work to find a new religion conceived "within the limits of simple reason" (*innerhalb der Grenzen der bloßen Vernunft*: "We [uphold Fichte in a Kantian tone] have of God only the moral concept given by pure practical reason").[9]

---

[8] This would imply some confusion between Fichte and Kant since the latter authored in 1793 *Religion Within the Bounds of Bare Reason (Die Religion innerhalb der Grenzen der bloßen Vernunft).*

[9] J. G. Fichte, Versuch einer Kritik aller Offenbarung, (*Attempt at a Critique of All Revelation*) 1792; edited and translated in Italian by di M. Olivetti, *Saggio di una critica di ogni rivelazione,* (Bari: Laterza, 1998), pp. 96-97. "With regard to nature, God is not properly its legislator, but rather its engine, its determinant; nature is mere instrument, whereas the moral agent is simply God" (ibid., p. 18). "By each of our conscious disobedience, not only do we do something exceptional compared to the law, but we also deny reason in general; not simply we sin against a law that derived from reason, but rather against its first commandment" (ibid., p. 23). According to Fichte, one needs to reckon "God's will as cause of the moral law within us" (ibid., p. 26). On these themes, this author refers to E. Brito, *Theologie et université selon Fichte,* in "*Revue Théologique de Louvain,*" n. 35 (2004), pp. 3-21; A. Denker, Kant und Fichte. *Kann die Religion vernünftig sein?,* in "Fichte-Studien," n. 8 (1995), pp. 41-58. English translation by A. Carnesecchi.

However, there were some reservations—when not real shadows—in regard to Fichte's theoretical profile. If *An Attempt at a Critique of All Revelation* was the object of a certain polyphonic debate not devoid of openly opposing standpoints (even if all agreed on considering Fichte's text a good point of reference for a critical discussion), then his two following pamphlets in 1793 blatantly support the ideas of the French Revolution, together called *Revolutionary Writings* (*Revolutionsschriften*), which contained *Contribution to the Rectification of the Public's Judgement of the French Revolution* (*Beitrag zur Berichtigung der Urtheile des Publicums uber die französische Revolution*) and *Reclaiming Freedom of Thought* (*Zurückforderung der Denkfreiheit*), and had dangerously attracted censors' attention to him. In Fichte's work, the sharp-eyed censors glimpsed features of thought that was at the same time revolutionary, democratic, Jacobin, and a sworn enemy of the sociopolitical establishment.

Although the two texts had circulated in a rigorously anonymous form, their real authorship became almost immediately of public domain, so that Fichte, not without a bit of a stretch, was classified as a radical Jacobin. In his two *Revolutionary Writings,* it is superfluous to remind the reader that the author manifested such an open adhesion to the revolutionary principles that, as the critics noticed, "Fichte's attitude towards the French Revolution shall be actually described as a kind of enthusiasm that is both restrained and deep."[10] That very enthusiasm, the landing point of his political reflection, was identified by the then elderly Kant as a prophetic sign of "the constant progress of humanity towards a better future."[11]

---

[10] S. Azzaro, *Politica e storia in Fichte,* (Milan: Jaca Book, 1993), p. 13.

[11] I. Kant, Political Writings, *Whether the Human Race Is in Constant Progress Towards the Better?* "The revolution of a population rich in spirit that we have witnessed in our time can succeed or fail; it can be so full of misery and atrocities that a man who righteously thinks, if he could hope to merrily attain it by carrying it out a second time, he would decide not to attempt this experiment at such a high price – this revolution, I say, finds in the souls of all

Beyond the thorny question around Fichte's political stance on which we shall come back later, it is necessary to notice that the censors were not wrong at all to focus attention against the philosopher, if we consider that a generic, anti-adaptive, political expression as well as an enthusiastic opinion on the French Revolution's legitimation emerged from the two 1793 texts. Fichte's judgement on the French Revolution was of a such a eulogistic nature that, as Reinhard Lauth reminded us, in Fichte's *Contribution* "It is missing the second part, the

---

the people (that are not directly involved in this game) a *participation* on the level of desire that borders on enthusiasm and which manifestation involved some risks: A participation that therefore, cannot have any other cause than a moral disposition inherent in mankind," in I. Kant, *Ob das menschliche Geschlecht im beständigen Fortschreiten zum Besseren sei*, in Id., *Der Streit der Fakultäten*, 1797. On the matter of the enthusiasm with regard to Kant's *Geschichtsphilosophie*, see J. F. Lyotard, *L'enthusiasme. La critique kantienne de l'histoire*, 1986. In regard to the matter of the French Revolution in Kant's thought, this author refers to the following works: L. Friedländer, *Kant in seiner Stellung zur Politik*, in "Deutsche Rundschau," 1876, pp. 241-255; K. Vorländer, *Kant's Stellung zur Französischen Revolution*, in *Philosophische Abhandlungen. Hermann Cohen zum 70. Geburtstag (4. Juli 1912) dargebracht*, (Berlin: Cassirer, 1912), pp. 247-269; H. Reiss, *Kant and the Right of Rebellion*, in "Journal of the History of Ideas," n. 17 (1956), pp. 179-192; N. Bobbio, *Kant e le due libertà*, in Id., *Da Hobbes a Marx*, (Naples: Morano, 1965), pp. 147-163; Id., *Kant e la Rivoluzione francese* (1989), in Id., *L'età dei diritti*, (Turin: Einaudi, 1990), pp. 143-155; L. W. Beck, *Kant and the Right of Revolution*, in "Journal of the History of Ideas," n. 32 (1971), pp. 411-422; V. Verra, *La Rivoluzione francese nel pensiero tedesco dell'epoca*, in "Filosofia," n. 20 (1969), pp. 411-440; P. Burg, *Kant und die Französische Revolution*, (Berlin: Duncker & Humblot, 1974); G. Luf, *Freiheit und Gleichheit. Die Aktualität im politischen Denken Kants*, (New York: Springer, 1978); Z. Batscha, *Bürgerliche Republik und bürgerliche Revolution bei Immanuel Kant*, in J. H. Schoeps, I. Geiss (edited by), *Revolution und Demokratie in Geschichte und Literatur. Zum 60. Geburtstag von W. Grab*, (Braun: Duisburg, 1979), pp. 133-148; A. Tosel, *Kant révolutionnaire. Droit et politique*, 1988. In here, Kant takes up, by applying it to history, Christian theology's terminology that considers the sacrament as *signum rememorativum* (that reminds of something), *signum demonstrativum* (that demonstrates, in the present), and as *signum prognosticum* (that allows to know what it will be). According to Thomas Aquinas' definition, the sacrament is *rememorativum passionis Christi et divinae gratiae demonstrativum, et future prognisticum* (Summa Theologica, III, q. 60, a. 3c.). The historical signs that predict something make known to the historians and politicians what will happen. Kant deals with the rememorative, demonstrative, and prognostic signs even in chapter 39 of his *Anthropologie in pragmatischer Hinsicht*. English translation by A. Carnesecchi.

historical one, where the situation of the time needed to be discussed. The main interest was the judgment on the Revolution's legitimacy." [12] That is to say, the theoretical justification of French actions and, as a consequence, the opportunity—unrevealed in the core of Fichte's works—to extend the influence towards the whole world according to that cosmopolitan call that opens the *Contribution* ("The French Revolution seems to me important for the entirety of humanity"). Fichte writes with universalistic stigma:

> *Revolution, that for the moment embraces nothing but just a part of the individuals, is accomplished. It is characteristic of any revolution to get rid of the ancient contract and to form a new union with a new contract. Both of these are lawful in any revolution in which the one thing and the other happen in a legitimate way, namely by virtue of the free will.*

Because of his praise of the French Revolution as an emancipative moment for humanity—in Kantian manner— "from a cosmopolitan standpoint," it is not a surprise that those who intended to give the Jena chair to Fichte were restrained by the worries regarding the philosopher's political profile and his proximity to the revolutionary radicalism that, as we shall see, will affect—not in a marginal way—*The Vocation of the Scholar* and in general the elaboration of Fichte's *Wissenschaftslehre*.[13]

Since the very beginning, two factions were formed at the University of Jena: One made up of those who were worried about Fichte's positions and did not want him to fill the chair, and those at the polar opposite who, even though they did not

---

[12] R. Lauth, *Il pensiero trascendentale della libertà. Interpretazioni di Fichte*, ed. by M. Ivaldo (Milan: Guerini, 1996), p. 308. English translation by A. Carnesecchi.
[13] J. G. Fichte, Contributo per rettificare i giudizi del pubblico sulla Rivoluzione francese, p. 162.

share the radicalism of the philosopher, wanted him to be part of the teaching body at Jena at any cost, to such an extent that they were even ready to soften the most bitter and radical traits of his theoretical positions. For example, Gottlieb Hufeland, professor of Law at Jena who belonged to this second group, claimed that Fichte was indeed a Democrat, but only law-wise, in an abstract way, without any concrete practical-political implication.[14]

The very same Christian Gottlieb von Voigt, grand-ducal official responsible for the university, expressed his perplexity upon the arrival of Fichte, wishing that the new professor would have soon softened or, even better, abandoned his pernicious "democratic fantasy." Because of this growing concern, on the May 18th, 1794, on the occasion of Fichte's arrival at Jena, von Voigt recommended Hufeland to cooperate so that the philosopher could dismiss without hesitation his odd democratic fantasies and in general, his political passion. Then he would exclusively commit to his teaching career and academic life with detached contemplation of any transforming wish. In short, the authorities asked Fichte—even if in a soft and open way—about his normalization and, as we shall see, especially the dismissal of his role of intellectual in order to take on the one of a mere scholar as a simply learned person, without any concrete link with the society and politics of his time. The intentions were clear and can be seen in the attempt of integrally neutralizing Fichte's political expressiveness by completely absorbing him in the institutional establishment. Fichte was expected to function as a symbolic doubling of the state of things as had, in part, happened with Schiller. The latter, made professor at Jena in 1789, had to abandon his revolutionary and tyrannicidal passion to then reconcile with

---

[14] Interesting hints in this respect can be found within the very documented monographic study by B. Bourgeois, *Philosophie et droits de l'homme de Kant à Marx*, (Paris: PUF, 1990). See also the excellent collection of J.G. Fichte's work, the *Lettres et témoignages sur la Révolution française*, ed. by I. Radrizzani, (Paris: Vrin, 2002), as well as its excellent introduction.

the *status quo,* of which he had become more and more an integral part.

The reference to Schiller is not a heteroclite coincidence if one considers that at Jena, the latter had not only completed this normalizing turn, but that Fichte in the very same university instead rejected this turn. In 1795, by publishing *On the Aesthetic Education of Man (Briefe uber die ästhethische Erziehung des Menschen),* Schiller's title politically opposed Fichte's lectures on the scholar's vocation.[15] It is particularly significative that in his *Briefe,* Schiller acknowledged the maximum expression of his time's negativity in that sectorial specialization culminating with, in his view, the division in estates which Fichte instead, in his *Vocation of the Scholar,* praises as a *condicio sine qua non* of the progress of humanity as a community.

Contrary to what had happened with Schiller, the authorities' wishes regarding Fichte would quickly prove delusive. Not only by keeping his distance from any kind of normalization, Fichte also had not introjected power's asymmetries and a resigned acceptance of actuality's logic, but the philosopher had also started off a course of additional lectures, which were open to anyone. *De officiis eruditorum* had at its core the political function of the intellectual as master and pedagogue of humanity, guide of a democratic and sympathetic human community towards its emancipation from power and other forms of submission to external forces in regard to the autonomous reason. The revolutionary ideas were not rejected but, in a totally opposite way, embodied in a larger framework of a theory of emancipation of mankind guided by culture, and thereon, by that particular estate, the intellectuals of which they were the holders. Also, the very *Wissenschaftlehre* that developed upon this basis became more and more clearly the philosophy of freedom of humankind, thought as solely acting subjectively in view of a full

---

[15] Luigi Pareyson, *Etica ed estetica in Schiller,* (Milan: Mursia, 1983), p. 158. English translation by A. Carnesecchi.

correspondence with itself. It is possible to legitimately claim with Buhr that "Fichte's relation with the French Revolution does not change, neither after his call at the University of Jena," as he remains faithful to the ideal which more than any other had animated the Revolution, nor had the possibility of transforming through action actuality's morphology, in view of a rationality still missing from the structures of reality.[16]

From this perspective, the five lectures on *The Vocation of the Scholar* are a splendid example of refusal of any resigned acceptance (*Anpassung*) firmly imposed by power and, in a symmetrical way, a demand for freedom of thought and of emancipative practices in the framework of a pragmatic and political conception of philosophy, as an unceasing attempt to make objective reality correspond to the reason of the social subjectivity of the human community. Since Fichte did not dismiss the revolutionary ideas but instead metabolized them through his explosive philosophy of praxis, his arrival at Jena was therefore:

A resounding beginning of his academic career. But such a debut, sided with the rumour of his political stance and a growing attention towards his persona for his lectures on the Wissenschaftslehre, ended up turning into a kind of burning mirror."[17]

Among Fichte's most enthusiastic listeners, Hölderlin wrote in November 1794: "Fichte is now the soul of Jena. And praise be to God that he is. I have never before known a man of such depth and energy of spirit."[18]

---

[16] Manfred von Buhr, *Revolution und Philosophie. Die französische Revolution und die ursprüngliche Philosophie Fichtes*, p. 94. English translation by A. Carnesecchi.

[17] C. De Pascale, *Etica e diritto: la filosofia pratica di Fichte e le sue ascendenze kantiane*, (Bologna: Il Mulino, 1995), p. 15. English translation by A. Carnesecchi.

[18] F. Hölderlin, *Ausgewählte Briefe*, (Jena: Diederich, 1910), p. 96. In *Ambiguity in the Western Mind*, ed. by Craig J. N. De Paulo, Patrick A.

Without resorting to using encoded language or diplomatic compromises, Fichte sent to the authorities an adamantine and unconditional message of opposition. Not only did he not want to submit to the will of the power, but also, he crossed the line by means of the series of incendiary lectures launched on May 23rd, 1793, the day of the first lesson on *The Vocation of the Scholar*. This heroic *modus operandi*, devoid of any will of compromise or of giving up, will accompany Fichte until 1799 when, with the epilogue of the atheism dispute (*Atheismusstreit*), the philosopher would leave his post following the accusation of atheism. Instead, however, what the institution could not stand was his emancipative democratism.[19] It is also true that, as had been underlined, in Fichte's reflection "There was no space for the notion of God as an essence or a being, whereas there was a unique activity, the one of the *I*, of the subject"—the unique guarantee of the world's moral order *(moralische Weltordnung)*—according to a line of thought that, strictly speaking, not only did not present any friction with the previous *Critique of all Revelation*, but instead seemed to be its most coherent fulfillment. [20] Nevertheless, as Fichte was very well aware, the accusation of atheism was just the paint that covered the unappealable condemnation of his ultra-democratic political positions.

In 1812, Fichte would prove once more he had a noble and free spirit. On that occasion, Fichte resigned from the post of Dean of the University of Berlin because of the conflict that placed him in opposition to the academic senate of the

---

Messina, Marc Stier, (California: Peter Lang, 2005), p. 157. English translation by A. Carnesecchi.

[19] Because it is not possible here to linger on the, even though essential, matter of the atheism dispute (and on the consequences that it had on Fichte's conceptual elaboration), this author just refers to the following studies devoted to topic: J. Rivera de Rosales, ed. by Ó. Cubo, *La polémica sobre el ateísmo. Fichte y su época*, (Madrid: Dykinson, 2009); Y. Estes, C. Browman, *J.G. Fichte and the Atheism Dispute (1798-1800)*, (Burlington: Ashgate, 2010); G. Ghia, *Fichte nella teologia: dall'Atheismusstreit ai giorni nostri*, (Milan: Guerini, 2003).

[20] C. Cesa, *J.G.Fichte e l'idealismo trascendentale*, (Bologna: Il Mulino, 1992), p. 21.

university. This was following the events in which he took the side of a Jewish student unjustly humiliated by a colleague who belonged to a wealthy and powerful family, as the latter was supported by the majority of the senate.

The 1794 lectures on the scholar that took place every Friday from six to seven p.m. were tremendously successful since the very beginning. Their success revealed how important Fichte's topics were perceived to be by the public; in particular, the role of culture in society as a possible way to transform the structure of power in view of a rationality still missing. On the other hand, the success could do nothing but reinforce the concern of authorities and professors who had meanwhile received confirmation of Fichte's ultra-democratic position. Fichte himself did not expect such a triumph as demonstrated by the active interest of his audience, inasmuch as the lecture hall was so packed that the public had to occupy the corridor as well as the courtyard to take part at the meetings.

With blatant satisfaction, on May 26th, 1794 Fichte wrote to his wife Johanna Rahn: "The biggest lecture hall in Jena's was too small, the corridor and the courtyard were packed, on desks and tables people were literally one on top of another."[21]

In the following lectures that took place weekly, the audience did not decrease. The second lesson concerning *Man's Vocation Within Society* took place on May 30th, the third one *The Difference between Estates within Society* on June 6th, while the fourth lesson, *The Scholar's Vocation* was on June 13th. The last one, *An Examination of Rousseau's Claims Concerning the Influence on Human Welfare of the Arts and Sciences*, was held on June 20th. Since the third lesson, the authorities had focused their attention on Fichte, labeling him as a revolutionary preacher who used his lectures to spread Jacobin messages, along with the idea that freedom is achievable through a revolutionary praxis that is meant to crush any form of resistance along the way. This was the only

---

[21] J.G. Fichte, *Briefwechsel. Kritische Gesamtausgabe*, ed. by H. Schulz, 2 voll., (Leipzig, 1925), I, p. 352. English translation by A. Carnesecchi.

possible outcome that, on the sociopolitical level, descended from the principles of *Wissenschaftslehre*. Therefore, from the very specific lectures that Fichte held in parallel for the students of philosophy, the authorities targeted the offices of learning (*De officiis eruditorum*) lectures because on the one hand, the massive participation of the public had raised some concern in the establishment, and on the other hand, their openly anti-adaptive, if not directly revolutionary message was incommensurably more evident. In this case, the all-encompassing (*toto genere*) sociopolitical perspective of Fichte's message was not in any way mediated by the sophisticated categorical apparatus of the *Wissenschaftslehre,* as it was the foundation from which the message arose.

Since December 1794, Friedrich Karl Forberg had highlighted the revolutionary-practical character of Fichte's lectures at Jena, noticing that the real goal of the philosopher's ontology of praxis, an outcome of the French Revolution, was the transformation of the existing system.

> *Fichte does really mean to operate in the world through his philosophy. The unsettled praxis' tendency that lives in every heart of a young person is diligently fed and cultivated by him so that, in this way, it will bear fruit in his time. Every occasion is good for him to inculcate the idea, according to which, to act is man's vocation.*[22]

This continuity, compared to the theoretical line developed in the *Contribution* and in the *Reclaiming Freedom of Thought,* could only appear blatant. In his *Revolutionary Writings,* by metabolizing some of Rousseau's starting points on popular sovereignty, Fichte upheld that peaceful reforms were preferable as a possible means of an irenical overcoming of the contradictions of the present time. However, he also expressly

---

[22] K. Forberg, *Fragmente aus meinen Papieren,* (Jena: Voigt, 1796), p. 30. English translation by A. Carnesecchi.

admitted that, in this case, the constant process of emancipation of mankind was hindered by the power structures in their despotic forms, and that this emancipative process, like gas pressurized in a tank, would explode, breaking the tank and destroying any surrounding reality, exactly like the 1789 revolution: a legitimate reaction of mankind to the obstacles preventing its free development oriented towards the future. With the unmistakable words of the *Reclaiming Freedom of Thought*, which were already a prelude to the infinite effort needed in order to overcome the obstacles codified in the *Wissenschaftslehre* in his first versions:

Humanity had to be miserable, but had not to remain such. Its political constitutions, source of the common misery, could certainly not be better (otherwise they would be already), but they must always become better and better. This happened during the time that we can trace back in the history of humanity before us and that will keep on happening as long as there would be a history of mankind, in one of these two ways: either through violent jumps or through a gradual progress, slow, but safe. By means of violent jumps, with great shakings, and social turmoil, a population may, in half of a century, advance more than it would otherwise have done in ten centuries. But this half of century is also miserable and full of sufferings, and this very same population can bounce back to the barbarity of a millennium before. The history of the world has evidences of both processes. The violent revolutions are always a daring shot for humanity; if they succeed, the victory fully compensates the distress they caused; if they fail, everything collapses into a bigger misery. More secure is to gradually proceed towards a greater progress of the light of reason and from thereon, towards the improvement of the political constitution. In such a scenario, the progress that you make is less considerable, while unfolding it; but look behind yourselves and you can see a long stretch of road that has already been covered.[23]

The theme of the revolutionary action which is at the core of the *Contribution* and of the *Reclaiming Freedom of Thought* also diagonally crosses the *Vocation of the Scholar*'s lectures, even though in a more cautious, dissimulated, though not less intense way. The duty of humanity is a never-ending process of emancipation, and its progress unfolds through society's overcoming of such obstacles according to the rhythm of history. Thereon, any force that hindered, slowed down, or stopped such process would be *ipso facto* illegitimate, and therefore, it would deserve destruction by means of radical and violent forms.

The perspective that has been adopted, as we can see, is always the *Contribution*'s and *Reclaiming Freedom of Thought*'s one, and it will remain so even after more or less fundamental adjustments are made until the end of Fichte's theoretical activity. In the *Wissenschaftslehre*—and in a more blatant way in the 1794-1795 *Foundations of Natural Right* matured almost at the same time as the *Vocation of the Scholar)*—Fichte's thought will find its solid theoretical foundation. Through a proper translation in philosophical concepts, the legitimacy is posited as an always reiterative, never-ending overcoming of obstacles put in place by human subjectivity.

The authorities' concerns were, therefore, reasonable yet completely delusive in their expectations of the possibility of "normalizing" Fichte's ideas. Suddenly, at Jena there were

---

[23] J. G. Fichte, *Zurückforderung der Denkfreiheit von den Fürsten Europens die sie bisher unterdrückten. Eine Rede*, 1793; tr. it. Ed. by V. E. Alfieri, *Rivendicazione della libertà di pensiero dai principi dell'Europa che l'hanno finora calpestata. Discorso, in Id., Sulla Rivoluzione francese. Sulla libertà di pensiero*, p. 7. See also C. De Pascale, *Vivere in società, agire nella storia. Libertà, diritto, storia in Fichte*, (Milan: Guerini, 2001), p. 6. Upon these topics, see also S. Azzaro, *Politica e storia in Fichte*, pp. 58 ss.; Id., *Sul pensiero politico-giuridico di G.A. Fichte*, in "*Rivista internazionale di filosofia del diritto*," 4.75 (1998), pp. 139-151. English translation by A. Carnesecchi.

rumours that the thinker from Rammenau was a subversive Jacobin who went about preaching that, in about twenty or thirty years, all the kings and princes would end up extinguished and that the people would become sovereign. On the other hand, one must not forget that in the German area, the term "Jacobin" enclosed several meanings that do not always converge. "Jacobin" not only referred to the French Revolution, but also by extension referred to any democratic orientation (even in the most pacific forms) or, in any case, to any political passion not embeddable in the chorus of the virtuous apologists of the system. From this perspective, Fichte's so-called "Jacobinism" must be carefully contextualized; otherwise, one may run the risk of falling into misleading interpretations of a different kind. Fichte was certainly a Democrat who did not reject revolution as an extreme measure *(extrema ratio)*; however, he was certainly not altogether a Jacobin because of his resolute refusal of the principles of the Enlightenment *(Aufklärung)*, even if it is undeniably present, especially in the 1796 writings, on the natural law of strong connections with Jacobin politics.[24]

The philosopher's detractors, in order to discredit and show Fichte's theoretical and practical dangerousness, tagged him as a Jacobin, highlighting his full adhesion to the principle of the revolution in its most radical declination. In 1795, for example, the reactionary newspaper *"Eudaemonia"* in its review of the second part of the *Contribution*, explicitly compared the German philosopher to Robespierre by defining Fichte as a "patriarch of the German sans-culottes," and his writings as "gospel of the beheaders," which maliciously

---

[24] On this point, see Manfred Buhr, *Revolution und Philosophie. Die französische Revolution und die ursprüngliche Philosophie Fichtes*, p. 44: "There are links, points of connection between Fichte and Robespierre (and the Jacobins) not only in *The Closed Commercial State*, but in Fichte's production from the beginning to the end: in his 1793 *Contribution*, with the juridical foundation of the use of revolutionary violence against the anti-revolutionary attempts, and then in the 1796/97 Foundation of Natural Right, with the formulation of the right of revolution and in the social matters." English translation by A. Carnesecchi.

presented the philosopher as a theoretical defender of the French guillotine in the German area.

In the meantime, in the ears of Jena's authorities the brave words of *Reclaiming Freedom of Thought* kept on resounding. Fichte openly claimed against every authority the inalienable right of freedom of thought and expression that he, himself, in 1794, did not intend to give up in his lectures, stating "On our freedom of thought, you princes do not have any *right* at all, no *faculty* to decide what is true and what is false, no right to determine the objects and the limits of our research."[25]

The truth cannot depend upon authorities, but can instead—this is the anti-Hobbesian corollary—become an incentive to react to the falseness of a power that opposes the goal of free development of humanity. This is a theme that in a more explicit way (if it is even possible) will be the core of *The Foundations of Natural Right* (1796) which followed.[26]

In the face of the more and more pressing accusations that outraged and quickly liquidated Fichte as a mere Jacobin, the philosopher energetically answered, as he used to, with a radical decision. He decided to publish his text on *Wissenschaftslehre* without changes or sweetening, in the exact form in which he edited his oral presentations that resulted in the accusation of Jacobinism. This was a reaction that, because

[25] J. G. Fichte, *Rivendicazione della libertà di pensiero dai principi dell'Europa che l'hanno finora calpestata. Discorso (Reclamation of the Freedom of Thought from the Princes of Europe, Who Have Oppressed It Until Now)*, cit., pp. 32-33. Cfr. W. Schulz, Johann Gottlieb Fichte: Vernuft und Freiheit, Neske, Pfullingen 1962, pp. 67.

[26] J. G. Fichte, *Grundlage des Naturrechts nach Principien der Wissenschaftslehre*, 1796; trans. by di L. Fonnesu, *Fondamento del diritto naturale secondo i principi della dottrina della scienza*, (Laterza: Roma-Bari, 1994). Here, it is not possible to linger, if not just tangentially and by few hints, on Fichte's foundation of *The Foundations of Natural Right* and its fundamental correlation with the theoretical structure of the *Doctrine of Science* (as well as on the theoretical consequences that arise from it). This author, therefore, refers to M. Baur – F. Neuhouser, *Fichte: Foundations of Natural Right*, Cambridge University Press, Cambridge 2000; D. Breazeale – T. Rockmore, *Rights, Bodies, and Recognition. New Essays on Fichte's Foundations of Natural Right*, (Burlington: Ashgate, 2006).

of his resoluteness, seemed to anticipate Fichte's decision a few years later when he was accused of atheism (*Atheismusstreit*). He firmly answered the accusations and after having gained the support of his students, resigned from his post at the University of Berlin. The analogy with the atheism dispute is relevant because on that occasion, as Fichte bitterly noticed, the accusation of atheism was nothing but the paint that hid a much more radical accusation against the political position of the philosopher, directed against his adherence to the cause of humanity which, guided by the intellectuals, freely acts upon and emancipates itself. "They are not after my atheism, but my democratism," Fichte wrote, referring to the atheism dispute case that undoubtedly marks a decisive moment in the transition of the work and life of the author.[27] As effectively, Luca Fonnesu underlined:

Since 1798, a whole series of events led Fichte to a deep rethinking of his philosophy. The abandonment of the chair of Jena following the accusation of atheism in 1798 marks for the thinker the end of a period of great influence on the cultural life and philosophical debate of the time. In the following years, Fichte's reservations start to arise also upon the French Revolution; if not for the "principles," at least for the "praxis." Even Kant, author of that revolution that Fichte and his contemporary had matched to the French one, publicly claims that Fichte's philosophy is "a system altogether unsustainable." Moreover, Fichte's rupture with Schelling will not delay, and it will be Schelling himself to substitute Fichte, and

---

[27] J. G. Fichte, *Scritti di una giustificazione giuridica*, in Id., *La dottrina della religione*, ed. by G. Moretto, (Naples: Guida, 1989), p. 170; in *Gesamtausgabe der Bayerischen Akademie der Wissenschaften* (= *GA*), ed. by di R. Lauth and H. Jacob, Fromman-Holzboog, (Cannstatt: Stuttgart-Bad), I, 6, p. 59. English translation by A. Carnesecchi.

therefore, to become the new guiding star in the conscience of the intellectuals.[28]

In the preface of the lectures on the intellectual, Fichte explicitly highlights the external "motive" which had led him to publish the text of the five lectures as he had prepared it for his presentation "without the alteration of a single word." The circumstance he refers to is actually the accusation and unwanted attention from authorities. As an inherent reaction to the censorship's promptness, *The Vocation of the Scholar* was published the very same year (1794) by Christian Ernst Gabler, editor in Jena and Leipzig. The reason for this choice was not only the free distribution of his idea of the intellectual who works with the social community with a view towards the constant evolutionary progress of the latter, but also a circumstantial goal to demonstrate how the accusations of being a sinister Jacobin revolutionary completely lacked any foundation.

In truth, Fichte's demonstration through the publication of the *Vocation of the Scholar* was not completely successful. Against them, Fichte demonstrated in his lectures how—now that everybody was able to assess them without the misleading accounts of the authorities—his process of rejuvenation (*Verjüngung*) of the world could happen in a pacific way, with the consent of humanity as a whole and without the bloodshed that had stained the French Revolution which was a legitimate process, even if not wise in regard to its concrete realization.[29] In the light of what had been said, Philonenko's words acquired a particular meaning: "In 1794, Fichte's lectures on *The*

---

[28] Luca Fonnesu, *Antropologia e idealismo. La destinazione dell'uomo nell'etica di Fichte*, (Rome-Bari: Laterza, 1993), p. 21. English translation by A. Carnesecchi.
[29] On the matter of democratism and rejuvenation of the world at the core of Fichte's politics (even in the last phase of Fichte's theoretical elaboration), see M. Gawlina, *Grundlegung des Politischen in Berlin. Fichte's späte Demokratie-Theorie in ihrer Stellung zur Antike und Moderne*, (Berlin: Duncker & Humblot 2002).

Vocation of the Scholar were a source of incidents. Fichte provokes his adversaries as much as their adversaries provoke him."[30]

It is significant that Fichte titled his work *Some Lectures on the Vocation of the Scholar (Einige vorlesungen uber die Bestimmung des Gelehrten)*. This title reveals that the philosopher had planned to keep on researching and developing the theme of the intellectual's ontology of praxis within society. Far from being an exposition in an accomplished and definitive form, these lectures might have been at first a provisory achievement or, if you want, a premise in view of further researching. Even from this perspective, it then becomes possible to uphold that *The Vocation of the Scholar*, more than an accomplished work, is instead a Foucaultian "node within a network" within a galaxy of heteroclite texts, open topics, and debates from which we need to draw the general "function of expression," placing a dynamic connection one with another.

That the 1794 lectures were, in Fichte's view, a starting point and not a landing one is also proved by the fact that, during the following academic semester between November 1794 and February 1795, when *The Vocation of the Scholar* had already been printed and encountered a large diffusion, the philosopher held other meetings on similar topics. These conferences, strictly speaking, were nothing but a prosecution of the previous course, a development of topics that had already been drafted and thereon, needed to be tabulated, recalibrated, and contextualized by new perspectives, always keeping in touch with the theoretical acquisitions linked to the development of the *Wissenschaftslehre*'s structure. Because there were no available hours in the university's weekly calendar, Fichte decided once again, with courage and determination, to book his lecture on a Sunday.

---

[30] Alexis Philonenko, *La liberté humaine dans la philosophie de Fichte*, (Paris: Vrin, 1966), p. 18. English translation by A. Carnesecchi.

His choice was immediately contested in a way that proved the demonstrative publication of *The Vocation of the Scholar* was unsuccessful, since Fichte had meant to demonstrate the substantial innocence of the text compared to the supine acceptance of Jacobin violence as the only possible means of emancipation. Fichte's detractors, even after the publication of the previous lectures, kept on seeing in him an insidious democratic Jacobin. A frontal attack on him ensued, claiming that his choice of holding the lectures on a Sunday hid, in a perfect Jacobin style, a deceitful tactic aimed at interfering with the public's religion and worship. The situation would have undoubtedly degenerated by potentially culminating in Fichte's expulsion from the academic body if the Grand Duke had not come to the rescue, allowing the philosopher to continue undisturbed with his public conferences in 1794. Their topic was *Concerning the Difference between the Spirit and the Letter within Philosophy (Uber den Unterschied des Geistes und des Buchstabens in der Philosophie)*.[31]

In continuity with *The Vocation of the Scholar*, the first lecture is about the public benefit of philosophy and the duty of the intellectual as a guide for human beings within society through employing social and political culture. The theoretical horizon upon which this first lecture moves asserts that, without philosophy, one could certainly live well by only dealing with economic matters at a time when an individual's existence could be considered accomplished even if lived in isolation from the social fabric.

In such a context, society was not conceived of as an ethical community of rational beings in constant interaction. The underlying idea that the demonization of metaphysics in Fichte's time was directly linked to the absolute of economics according to a motif that will widely unfold in Fichte's following texts, finding its maximum expression in 1800 with *The Closed*

---

[31] See J.G. Fichte, *Über den Unterschied des Geistes und des Buchstabens in der Philosophie*, 1794; tr. it. ed. by U.M. Ugazio, *Sullo spirito e la lettera*, (Turin: Rosenberg & Sellier, 1989).

Commercial State (*Der geschlossene Handelsstaat*) and in his 1808 *Addresses to the German Nation* (*Reden an die deutsche Nation*). In *Concerning the Difference between the Spirit and the Letter within Philosophy*, Fichte summons and develops in different perspectives the topic—architrave of the *Vocation of the Scholar*—of the intellectual as a master of humanity who maintains and monitors mankind's progress thanks to the knowledge of the destination, the means, and the difficulties that such an itinerary implies. Far from being abandoned as a research that has already been accomplished, the topic of the lectures upon the scholar finds therefore, in the *Difference between the Spirit and the Letter within Philosophy* an additional moment of in-depth analysis.

Fichte will come back to the matter of the intellectual and his role as educator of humankind twice, testifying to both the importance of the topic in his reflection and the temporal nature of the theoretical acquisitions achieved during his conferences in 1794.[32] In 1806, Fichte will print ten lectures *On the Essence of the Scholar and its Appearance in the Realm of Freedom* (*Uber das Wesen des Gelehrten und seine Erscheinungen im Gebiete der Freiheit*) delivered the year before at the University of Erlangen, as a new and improved edition of the 1794 conferences. Then in 1812, the philosopher will publish *Five Lectures on the Vocation of the Scholar* (*Fünf Vorlesungen uber die Bestimmung des Gelehrten*), resulting from the course's hold upon this topic in the 1811 summer semester at the University of Berlin, summoning and further developing once again this category previously drafted in the 1794 course. It is not then surprising that in the short preface of the 1794 *The Vocation of the Scholar* edition, Fichte presented them as an "introduction to a whole which the

---

[32] On the topic of the *Bestimmung des Gelehrten* after 1794 in Fichte's works and thought; see also *Zur "Bestimmun des Gelehrten" nach der späten Wissenschaftslehre Fichtes*, in "*Vierteljahrsschrift für wissenschaftliche Pädagogik*," n. 65 (1989), pp. 426-440.

Author intends to complete and when the time permits, lay before the public."[33]

As Buhr pointed out, the fact that Fichte delivered lectures on the scholar's vocation in every phase of his philosophy and in every university in which he taught proves the intimate unity of his thought against the so-called "turns" as well as the so-called "changes of paradigm."[34] In a converging way, it also values the thesis, according to which such unity can be found in the two inseparable theoretical intersections of particular versus universal, in view of the emancipation of mankind (the estate of the intellectuals being the only possibility of humanity's emancipation) and in the relation of praxis versus thought as a fundamental problem of Fichte's thought. With Buhr's own words, "the ideal model for Fichte was to bring together speculation and action" in the form of the scholar, as well as in the ideal of a culture that immediately overflows with an energy capable of permeating and shaping society.[35]

There is an unexpected analogy existing between the project of *The Vocation of the Scholar* and the one regarding the *Wissenschaftslehre*. On the one hand, this analogy seems to sketch how both lines of research were for Fichte two problems, to such an essential extent that these will prompt him to redefine them for his entire life, as well as a prospect for new actualization according to the constant work of improvement fully coherent within the structure of the *Wissenschaftslehre* itself. On the other hand—and here lies the most interesting aspect for us—the existing analogy between the scholar's vocation and *Wissenschaftslehre* also highlights how, between the two types of research apparently led without any point of tangency along two different lines of theoretical philosophy and political philosophy, there is a game of references so fruitful

[33] J.G. Fichte, *The Vocation of the Scholar*, Introduction, Wikisource.
[34] M. Buhr, *Revolution und Philosophie. Die französische Revolution und die ursprüngliche Philosophie Fichtes*, pp. 15. English translation by A. Carnesecchi.
[35] Ibid., p. 16. English translation by A. Carnesecchi.

and intense as to make one think that, in the end they were nothing but two articulations of the very same reflections—in themselves unitary—albeit developed according to differentiated perspectives. In this sense, one can legitimately claim, by following (and integrating) Buhr's own words:

> *The vocation of the scholar's doctrine of knowledge, natural law, and ethical system from a unitary structure are different moments of the same thing...[because] the destination of Fichte's efforts in all the spheres of his philosophy is the same: the theoretical foundation of man's autonomous activity in view of the development of human dignity through the ethical law in accordance with man's social relationships.[36]*

In this lies the expressive unitary function of Fichte's web of thoughts, beyond the galaxy of his works and the changes of perspective in which they take shape.

In this respect, this author intends to take the distances from two interconnected—and not at all secondary—aspects highlighted by Cesa in his important work *J.G. Fichte and the Transcendental Idealism* (*J.G. Fichte e l'idealismo trascendentale*, 1992). On the one side, by referring to Fichte's theoretical profile, Cesa explains that "revolutionary and national ideas are not the key to understand [Fichte's] philosophy."[37] On the other side, in 1794 the scholar's vocation "is not in contrast with the theoretical structure of *Wissenschaftslehre*, but does not at all depend on it."[38] In a diametrically opposed way (and partially converging with Buhr's position), this author will try to demonstrate how Fichte's philosophy originated from the specific political and social context of the time—in particular from the "axial"

[36] Ibid., p. 107. English translation by A. Carnesecchi.
[37] Claudio Cesa, *J.G.Fichte e l'idealismo trascendentale*, p. 16. English translation by A. Carnesecchi.
[38] Ibid., p. 199.

experience of the French Revolution—and how the 1794 lessons on the *Vocation of the Scholar* depend in a symbiotic way on the structure of the *Wissenschaftslehre* of which they are the most coherent development on the level of the sociopolitical praxis (especially, as we shall see, regarding the third principle as unfolded by the 1794-1795 *Basis of Natural Law*).[39]

It is, after all, Fichte who suggests it: The second lecture on the scholar opens with the theoretical call to the necessity found in *State Education and Science (Staat, Erziehung und Wissenschaft)* as a holistic knowledge of truth, in order to come to *Wissenschaftslehre*. In the third lecture, in order to give an account of the fragmentation of society, Fichte writes: "I have to, thereon, introduce some universal law drawn from *Wissenschaftslehre*."[40] It follows that, as in the title of the work on natural law (1796) and of the one on the system of ethics (1798), Fichte adds the specification in *According to the Principles of Science (nach Principien der Wissenschaftslehre)* in order to underline the existing link with the general theoretical structure. Also, the title of the text regarding the intellectual's vocation could be virtually completed with the same extension: *According to the Principles of Science*.

If, as Cesa himself suggests (at least partially contradicting his previous claim), "the most theoretical parts of those 'popular' writings as were defined by Fichte deserve to be put on the same level as the scientific treatises and therefore, to be read bearing always in mind the latter,"[41] this author believes that it is also true that the scientific parts must be put in relation with the popular ones, and that both kinds must be

---

[39] Upon this topic, see also Enrico Martini's translation, comment and contextualization of *The 1881 Scholar's Vocation* by putting them in a direct connection with the 1810 *Wissenschaftslehre*. See also J.G. Fichte, *Lezioni sulla destinazione del dotto (1811)* and *La dottrina della scienza, esposta nel suo profilo generale (1810)*, ed. by. E. Martini, (Milan: Mimesis, 2011).

[40] J.G. Fichte, *The Vocation of the Scholar*, III lecture: "*The Distinction of Classes in Society.*"

[41] C. Cesa, *J.G. Fichte e l'idealismo trascendentale*, p. 7.

referred to in the actual historical picture in which Fichte led his life and elaborated his philosophy. According to Buhr's suggestion that, in the present work it is integrally embraced as well as considered the polar star of Fichte's interpretation, "Fichte's thought must be, first of all, explained not starting from history of philosophy but from history as such."[42]

In this respect, it is not possible to agree with Pasquale Salvucci, according to whom Fichte landed at the matter of the social relationship and therefore, of the communitarian intersubjectivity only in 1796 with his work on the natural law. "From 1796 onward, Fichte moves from a philosophy of the "I" to a philosophy of the "we," because of the prevailing problem of the community."[43] This thesis is radicalized by Salvucci to such extent that he then claims: "The first presentation in 1794 did not even discern the problem of the genesis of the world of men, by resolving itself there, in the *not-I*."[44]

Carla Amadio's standpoint is instead, agreeable. In her study *Logic of the Political Relation. A Study on Fichte's Doctrine of Knowledge,*[45] she has shown how *The Basis of Natural Law* unfolds—not in a secondary way—the themes that are linked to the social, political, and communitarian dimension. After all, Amadio's thesis—which this author shares in its essential points—allows light to be shed on the contemporary presentation of the scholar's vocation which is the most coherent and effective codification of the sociopolitical *Wissenschaftslehre*'s vocation, and from Salvucci's perspective, is left unexplained or, at most, ends up being read in a completely independent way from the articulation of the *Wissenschaftslehre* (according to the hermeneutic way that can be also found in Cesa).

---

[42] M. Buhr, *Revolution und Philosophie. Die französische Revolution und die ursprüngliche Philosophie Fichtes*, p. 41.
[43] Pasquale Salvucci, *Dialettica e immaginazione in Fichte*, (Argalia: Urbino, 1963), p. 73. English translation by A. Carnesecchi.
[44] Ibid., p. 247. English translation by A. Carnesecchi.
[45] *Logica della relazione politica. Uno studio su "La dottrina della scienza (1794) di J.G. Fichte."* 1998

One can, after all, fruitfully claim that, like the *Wissenschaftslehre*, the essential sociopolitical related text that is the *Vocation of the Scholar* kept Fichte busy till the end of his life. This motif will come back with emphasis, even though in a theoretical framework not devoid of important novelties (mostly due to a historical context that had changed in the meantime). Even in the 1798 *Lectures on the Theory of Ethics* (*Sittenlehre*), which explains the role of the intellectual as a propagator of morality), in *The Closed Trading State (Der geschlossene Handelstaat)* with its codification of the intellectual as a defender of the human community against the international automatism of the market), in the *Characteristics of the Present Age* (*Grundzüge des Degenwärtigen Zeitalters*) in which there is the theorization of the intellectual as the people's guide in view of overcoming the "completed sinfulness" of the present age, and in the *Speeches to the German Nation* with their thematization of the intellectual as a warlord of the German nation against the French invader. [46]

Coherent with the overview of the galaxy of Fichte's works in those years, one cannot forget that Fichte, while delivering his conferences on the *Vocation of the Scholar*, had published as a programmatic text for his academic lectures to his philosophy students *Concerning the Conception of Doctrine of Knowledge Generally* (*Über den Begriff der Wissenschaftslehre*, 1794). It is particularly significant that—as a proof of what has been said while following Foucault's footsteps—in the appendix of this text there was an explicit reference to the public conferences upon the intellectuals' morality that Fichte recalled in order to show the direct connection to the sociopolitical fundamental principles of the *Wissenschaftslehre*.

---

[46] About this, see H.C. Engelbrecht, *Johann Gottlieb Fichte. A Study of his Political Writings with Special Reference to his Nationalism*, (New York: AMS Press, 1968); T. Harada, *Politische Ökonomie des Idealismus und der Romantik: Korporatismus von Fichte, Müller und Hegel*, (Berlin: Duncker und Humblot, 1989).

This was due to the (not indeed implicit) belief that the intellectuals, as they embodied among human beings the maximum achievement of knowledge, could—better than any other individual—be the bearers of that ontology of praxis aimed at the rationalization of the reality and the harmonization of the object with the active subject.[47] The latter aspect—soul of Fichte's entire project—finds its brightest expression in the third principle of the *Wissenschaftslehre* in the way it is presented in the 1794-1795 *The Basis of Natural Law* that, as Philonenko reminded us, is "the first authentic and coherent outlook of the world" sketched by Fichte.[48] More precisely, the work *Concerning the Conception of Doctrine of Knowledge Generally* significantly ends with the two-fold stress on the emancipative function of science (called to set free and make mankind self-conscious as well as conscious of its unity) and in a converging way, on the *Doctrine of Knowledge Generally* as the guide of mankind through culture:

> *It is more and more necessary to take to heart the following questions: What is the proper vocation of the scholar? In which place, in the order of things, does he find his place? In which kind of relation are the intellectuals among themselves and with the other human beings and, most of all, with each of the other's social classes? How and through which means can they continuously carry out their duties given to them by virtue of these relations? And how must they educate themselves on this ability? These are the questions that I disclosed during the public lectures under the denomination of morality for scholars which I will try to answer.[49]*

---

[47] On this theme, see K. Hammacher, *Transzendentale Theorie und Praxis: Zugänge zu Fichte*, (Amsterdam: Rodopi, 1996).
[48] Alexis Philonenko, *La liberté humaine dans la philosophie de Fichte*, p. 33. English translation by A. Carnesecchi.
[49] J.G. Fichte, *Concerning the Conception of Science of Knowledge Generally*, Wikisource, 1794. English translation by A. Carnesecchi.

In the following pages, we will focus on the alchemic relation existing between *The Scholar's Vocation* and *Wissenschaftslehre* (and more precisely, on the first one as a declination of the second one *sub specie communitatis* [under the appearance of the community]) in order to highlight the inner connection in the spirit of a praxis theoretically founded and socially practised. Firstly, however, we will need to focus on the scholar's profile drafted by Fichte in his *Vorlesungen* (lectures). On this point, Luigi Pareyson's considerations, according to which the *Wissenschaftslehre* was born in the form of "a translation in philosophical terms of both Christianity and Jacobinism," seem to be convincing. [50] In particular:

The welcoming of Kant's philosophy was in view of a philosophical re-valuation of Christianity and French Revolution's ideas. In such a way, in Fichte's thought the religious and political needs, finally formulated in the form of a philosophical problem and pacified in a reasoned solution, were blended and confused with each other into the ideal of a secular religion destined to renew human, civil, and political society through the work of a church of scholars. This is the problem from which Fichte's philosophy originated. It is in order to solve these issues that the first assumption of Fichte's thought is the definition of a "philosophy of freedom." [51]

In order to be fully unfolded on the worldly level, Fichte's philosophy of freedom needs the intellectuals" active intervention.

---

[50] Luigi Pareyson, second edition of *Fichte: il sistema libertà*, (Milan: Mursia, 1976), pp. 30-31. English translation by A. Carnesecchi.
[51] Ibid., p. 31. English translation by A. Carnesecchi.

♦

"The Scholar [here meant as intellectual] is destined in a peculiar manner for society: his estate, more than any other, exists only through society and for society."

J.G. Fichte, *The Vocation of The Scholar*

♦

"Not for idle contemplation of thyself, not for brooding over devout sensations; no, for action art thou here; thine action, and thine action alone, determines thy worth."

J.G. Fichte, *The Vocation of Man*

♦

2.

"Intellectual," not "Scholar"

♦

This author's decision to translate *The Vocation of the Scholar* may seem an arduous task, as well as odd and misleading, if not totally wrong. At first, it could appear that the text which Fichte consecrates to the labor of dismantling the traditional figure of the scholar, as well as complementary codification of the duties and the mission of such, defines the intellectual in the modern sense. As we will see, in the pages of Fichte's opus beats the heart of a project of rejuvenation of the world by a specific estate—the intellectuals—who act and think in direct opposition to the canonical *modus operandi* of the scholar, bearer of an "individual" knowledge, and devoid of any link with the surrounding sociopolitical actuality. Nevertheless, this decision is the result of a thoughtful choice, due to—it will be said right away—different reasons, both conceptual and editorial.

First of all, the choice can be explained by the fact it was preferable to remain within the Italian "history of the effects" (*storia degli effetti*) or the German "impact of history"

(*Wirkungsgeschichte*), and as such, in a stable and unitary way receive Fichte's text with the title *The Vocation of the Scholar* (*La missione del dotto*), the manner of which does not make any variation justifiable, no matter how motivated it may be. The title of the lectures on *The Vocation of the Scholar* is rendered in Italian by Carlo Mazzantini, Vittorio Enzo Alfieri, Nicolao Merker, Giacomo Perticone, Marco Marroni, Elsa Roncali, Giovanni Plinio Marotta Emilio Cassetti, and Nadia Cappelletti. [52] In the presence of such a stable as well as majestic tradition, the author could do nothing but maintain the original title *The Vocation of the Scholar*, trying to show in the following pages in which sense such title can be misleading in this age.

After all, the translation of the title *The Vocation of the Intellectual* would have been odd and moreover unjustified in front of such a stable tradition, not only for the reason that such a translation would have been openly in antithesis with the editorial tradition to which Fichte's work is firmly linked, but also because it would have substituted—in a not at all innocent way—the classic "scholar" with "intellectual." Namely, a figure which, strictly speaking at Fichte's time, had not yet even been codified and which aurorally takes shape in a clear and unmistakable way in the philosopher's text. This is the second reason—more properly conceptual—that has led this author to keep the canonical translation of the title on the conceptual level, even if it is undoubtedly unsatisfying.

Therefore, in the following pages it will be explained why, even though it has been chosen to maintain the traditional title, the profile drafted by Fichte not only does not fully correspond to the definition of "intellectual" as currently used,

---

[52] *La missione del dotto,* translated into Italian by Carlo Mazzantini (Turin: International Publishing society, 1932) Vittorio Enzo Alfieri (Padoa: Cedam, 1946), Nicolao Merker (Rome: Editori Riuniti, 1982), Giacomo Perticone (Turin: Paravia, 1935), Marco Marroni (Pordenone: Studio Tesi, 1991), Elsa Roncali (Lanciano: Carabba, 1912), Giovanni Plinio Marotta (Bergamo: Minerva Italica, 1969), Emilio Cassetti (Bari: Laterza, 1948) e Nadia Cappelletti (Florence: Le Monnier, 1965).

but it also blatantly excludes the opposite figure of the scholar as he is traditionally meant. If one focuses on Fichte's work, both components of *Some Lectures on the Vocation of the Scholar* and *Five Lectures on The Vocation of the Scholar* — because of their polysemous structure—need to be taken into consideration as the objects of a critical analysis. The first one, *Some Lectures* that will come back in the following work, *The Vocation of Man (Bestimmung des Menschen*, 1800), alludes to a rich galaxy of heterogeneous meanings with inter-connectedness between them, referring to at least three dimensions of "destination," "vocation," and "mission."[53] These three dimensions were already present in Johann Joachim Spalding's work, entitled *The Vocation of Man* (1748) that had a certain influence on Fichte himself.[54]

These three different determinations all virtually lie in the meaning that Fichte gives in his course to the figure of the scholar, inasmuch as (a) He is destined to take action in society and cannot perceive himself as an outsider. (b) By adhering to the idea of being destined, *The Vocation of the Scholar* answers to a "call," an inner "voice" (*stimme*) that guides him towards the goal for which he is preordained.[55] (c) In his answer and his loyalty towards the voice that calls him to his destination, *The Vocation of the Scholar* accomplishes his mission of guiding humanity painlessly towards approaching the achievement of unity with all humankind, namely to the never-ending self-

---

[53] On the polysemous determinations of the term *"Bestimmung"* in Fichte's lexicon, see P.L. Oesterreich, H. Traub, *Zur Semantik des Wortes "Bestimmung,"* in Idd., *Der ganze Fichte: die populäre, wissenschaftliche und metaphilosophische, und metaphilosophische Erschliessung der Welt,* Kohlhammer, (Stuttgart, 2006), pp. 267 on.

[54] J.J. Spalding, *Die Bestimmung des Menschen,* 1748; Italian translation ed. by G. Landolfi Petrone, *La vocazione dell'uomo,* (Bompiani: Milan, 2011). Upon the theme of the "vocation of man" before Fichte, see also G. Zöller, *Die Bestimmung der Bestimmung des Menschen bei Mendelssohn und Kant,* in V. Gerhardt et alii (ed. by), *Kant und die Berliner Aufklärung. Akten des 9. In ternationalen Kant-Kongresses (26. bis 31. Maerz 2000 in Berlin),* (Berlin: Gruyter, 2011), IV, pp. 476-489.

[55] The third lecture, as we will see, is wholly dedicated to the topic of the choice of estate as a vocation and thereon, as a free answer to a "call."

development (that distinguishing feature of human dignity [*dignitas hominus*], according to Pico della Mirandola's teachings, that codified the beginning of the modern era) leads to the full harmonization of humanity with its own ontological potentialities and the surrounding world.

In his rich commentary to the French edition of Fichte's work, *Conferences on the Destination of the Savant (Conférences sur la destination du savant)* (1794) (Paris: Vrin, 1969), Jean-Louis Vieillard-Baron effectively insisted upon the multiplicity of meanings that the word "vocation" bears in Fichte's work.[56] In this sense, because of its contextualization of Fichte's opus and its references to the theoretical structure of *Wissenschaftslehre*, one must keep in mind also the German edition by Reinhard Lauth with Hans Jacob and Peter Schneider, *Of the Duties of the Scholar, Jena lectures (Von den Pflichten der Gelehrten. Jenaer Vorlesungen 1794/95* (Hamburg: Meiner, 1971).

If the term vocation as meant by Fichte implicates the virtual coexistence of the three dimensions outlined just above—even though they are hidden behind the only apparent predominance of the second one—with regard to the word "scholar," there is instead that mutual elision between the two opposite determinations of the learned person and the intellectual that, as we will see, is for Fichte himself to outline on the theoretical level, albeit without a rigorous terminological distinction. The protagonist of the 1794 lectures is the intellectual as a figure counterposed to the scholar, traditionally meant as the bearer of a kind of knowledge that is disembodied from the social and political texture in its genesis as well as in its concrete realizations.

If we wanted to literally translate the German expression, scholar is the one who knows because he learned at school. He is namely the expert, the consultant, the one who has received education, the scholar (*De officiis eruditorum* is—as we have

---

[56] See J.-L. Vieillard-Baron, commentary, in J.G. Fichte, *Conférences sur la destination du savant (1794)*, (Paris: Vrin, 1969), pp. 94-96.

seen—the way in which the official calendar for Fichte's lectures was presented) is the man who culturally shaped himself through an apprenticeship and who devoted his existence to study and to culture. In Fichte, all those determinations fully coexist, but there is another essential super-determination (that is missing in the literal meaning of the word) which nevertheless, is unavoidable in order to fully understand the extent of the scholar as it is considered in Fichte's reflection. More precisely, this conceptual super-determination consists in the primarily practical, political, communitarian, and active—not exclusively theoretical—vocation that, from Fichte's point of view, characterizes the man of culture in its highest meaning, directly counterposing him to the old-fashioned scholar. The scholar is characterized instead by a *"pathos* of the distance" and by the complete absence of any practical-political activity in touch with the actual texture of the community of belonging.

The fact that, in all of the Italian editions of Fichte's work that have been published, until now the translation of "scholar" (in Italian *"dotto,"* from Latin *"eruditus"* and German *"gelehrter"*) has never been called into question and cannot be glossed over. This is due to an impeccably literary but conceptually misleading translation, not directly characterized by the ideological sense of the complete removal of praxis (according to the dominant ideology upon which the contemporary deserted landscape of the postmodern "complete sinfulness" was going to be shaped). The fact that Fichte's language had not yet distinguished in precise terminology the figure of the scholar from the intellectual does not mean the modern interpreter or translator should bypass this distinction. This is also in light of the fact that—we shall repeat—the existing polarity between the two profiles is widely argued by Fichte himself, even though not on the level of terminology. This is the keystone of the entire interpretation of *The Vocation of the Scholar* and *The Vocation of Man*, both in his 1794 lectures and from a different perspective in his following lectures devoted to the same topic.

Such a distinction between "the letter" and "the spirit" is, after all, deeply coherent with Fichte's discourse, inasmuch as he is the one who, in *On the Spirit and the Letter in Philosophy* (*Uber Geist und Buchstabe in der Philosophie*, 1795), tenaciously insists upon the heterogeneity between the two on the one hand, and on the other hand, insists on the hermeneutical necessity to understand the parts of a discourse by starting from the whole. Namely, it is the very spirit of this discourse which highlights in a symmetric and complementary way the existing circularity that ties the two together in the infinite expressions of the life of the spirit.

This is of a great theoretical significance because—applied to the same author—it allows us to decipher the conceptual difference existing between the scholar and the intellectual, It is for Fichte himself to posit on the theoretical level, even though not on the linguistic one (in the "spirit" but not in the "letter"), the fruitful hermeneutic circularity between the *Wissenschaftslehre*. As Foucault would put it, inherent in the polyhedral texts that form the net of Fichte's opus, the deep unity that connects them all together forms the determination of a unique system that can unfold on different levels. As a matter of fact, in the coherent distinction between "the spirit" and "the letter" within the different categories of thought (religious, political, esthetical, ethical, pedagogical) must refer to each other in a symphonic way in order to fully light up their autonomy. Their plurivocity call one to another, and together they refer to the common horizon that is *Wissenschaftslehre*: The firm foundation (*fundamentum inconcussum*) of Fichte's system—the nucleus from which arise all the heterogeneous permutations of his thought.

In Italian, scholar refers to an individual who has studied for a considerable time, acquiring wide and in-depth knowledge, who *ipso facto* is a learned person, a wise man— namely a person who, because of his theoretical choice, remains distant from the perilous lands of politics and action within society—and considers the latter a swerve from the goal *(telos)* of the acquisition of culture as part of an individual's theoretical formation. The word, after all, undoubtedly refers to the single person, to the competencies he has acquired as an individual—no matter the social or political context wherein he lives or by which he is educated—and which he could influence because of his competencies. The higher his level of education, the further he has to be from social and political life, isolated in the ivory tower of pure disembodied theory. That is what the function of the learned person traditionally meant. His culture is, thereon, a purely individual matter, devoid of the two-way nexus with reality which is the fundamental characteristic of the intellectual's mission which Fichte codified according to the give-and-take dialectic. Accordingly, the scholar is formed within the society by receiving culture from it, and also acts within society by giving to society a concrete contribution as a guide for mankind.

In other words, whilst the scholar believes he has not taken anything from society, instead, as Fichte expressively upholds, his culture is entirely conditioned by the social development and the tangible historical framework. Because of this error of assessment, the scholar also feels justified in not giving anything back to it. The intellectual, however, knows that he took his culture from the concrete social cosmos in which he lives. In this social context, the intellectual finds the actual meaning of his action that is aimed at transforming society in a way that provides the practical energy of culture. Culture concretizes the constant work of rationalization of reality and enhancement of humanity which coincides, strictly speaking, with the vocation of man, and therefore of the intellectual, as a man perfectly formed. From a different perspective, the scholar does not enable the interaction between knowledge and actual social framework, as his knowledge is not itself socially characterized or inextricably connected with society, politics, and community life.

By framing the issue in more specific terms, one can thereon uphold that the intellectual is the sociopolitical version of the scholar. It follows—in Fichte's view—that only the intellectual (the scholar's fullest actualization) can acquire a full comprehension of the practical-emancipative nature of culture, as well as the nexus that links culture to his own social and historical framework in outcomes no less than geneses. In the pages of *The Vocation of Man* (1800), this perspective will surface in a particularly gleaming way: "not merely *to know*, but according to thy knowledge, *to do* is thy vocation."[57] Then, "Not for idle contemplation of thyself, not for brooding over devout sensations—no, for action art thou here; thine action, and thine action alone determines thy worth."[58] These are passages of great interest because, besides reconfirming the intellectual's undoubtedly practical orientation of culture, they also support the evidence of the thesis—fully welcomed in this work—according to which the so-called "second Fichte," the one who comes after the "starting point" represented by *The Vocation of Man*, does not renounce his pragmatic vocation and previous acquisitions, but places them within a theoretical horizon characterized by indisputable rethinking and essential novelties.[59] Pareyson underlined this in the most effective way:

> *Fichte came at positing the absolute because of his very desire to give to human activity, permeated of divine life, a creative power much more intense and wider than the action confined in the ethical-juridical world, in order to reinforce man's action in the world so that he becomes*

---

[57] J.G. Fichte, *The Vocation of Man*, translated from German by William Smith, Wikisource, 1846.

[58] *Ibid.*

[59] Actually, at the present time, none of the academics openly consider the old thesis according to which Fichte's philosophy, after the nineteenth century, undergoes such a turn to then change *toto genere* its features. Nevertheless, the prejudice about the existence of "two" Fichtes completely kept separate by the threshold of *The Vocation of Man* (1800) keeps on being a prejudice that, for however rarely it is made explicit, is still firmly rooted. See Cesa, J.G. *Fichte e l'idealismo trascendentale*, pp. 42 ss.

*able to transform reality by redeeming it in a superior
unity with the divine life.*[60]

The concept of the absolute, thereon, neither neutralises nor
reduces Fichte's ontology of praxis; on the contrary, it does
intensify it by establishing it upon another foundation. About
what has been said so far, one cannot forget that in the Gospel
of John, which Fichte after 1800 (and especially, in a more
programmatic way, in his lectures on *The Way Towards the
Blessed Life*) will always refer to, Fichte finds at least three
decisive points interconnected with each other. He employs
them in order, not to "overcome" the structure of
Wissenschaftslehre, but rather to "reassert" it.[61] These points
are: (a) The ontological root of the creative love, namely the
absolutely free and unconditioned action that creates reality
without being determined by anything except its freedom. (b)
The absolute dependency of the world from its creator (of the
not-I from the *I*), namely the non-objectivity of the objective
world. (c) The social connection that links, through faith, the
subjects with each other and the Creator.

A man of culture in a modern sense, firmly plays the part of
the protagonist in the process of society's transformation, while
the intellectual is the individual who knows why he takes
action in society, and who takes action in society because he
knows and he is aware—his awareness is the always
reasserted fruition as well as the outcome of his knowledge—
that mere theory is totally insufficient, as *The Vocation of Man*
is to take action in society so that his own principles may find
actual citizenship within the folds of a community. By paving
the difficult way with efforts and regressions, difficulties and
setbacks, the never-ending enhancement of humanity is made
possible, so that society is more and more self-aware and
conscious of its ontological possibilities:

---

[60] L. Pareyson, *Fichte: il sistema della libertà*, p. 415. English translation by A. Carnesecchi.
[61] See C. Cesa, *Introduzione a Fichte*, (Rome-Bari: Laterza, 2008), pp. 171.

The scholar (meaning "the intellectual") is destined in a peculiar manner for society: his class, more than any other, exists only through society and for society: it is thus his peculiar duty to cultivate the social talents, an openness to receive, and a readiness to communicate knowledge, in the first place and in the highest degree.[62]

In favour of the present text's stance about the need of considering as an intellectual Fichte's scholar, one has also to consider the fact that the lectures on *The Vocation of the Scholar* were openly addressed to a heterogeneous and fragmented audience made up of intellectuals as well as common men called to synergistically cooperate in view of their ethical action through society. The very intellectual biography of Fichte is the most splendid evidence of the social role played by the scholar. The latter, complete in his way of being, is the bearer of a universal knowledge, and he is far enough from that "specialistic idiotism" that consisted, as Lukács well knew, in "that exact dissertation of pseudo-problems" cosmically distant from the comprehension of his own time in his thought and from the active praxis of rejuvenation (*Verjüngung*) of the world.[63]

---

[62] J.G. Fichte, *The Vocation of the Scholar*. For Fichte, the intellectual ought to be a living paradigm of such activities and must seek to promote them in society. The existing nexus between "giving" and "receiving" enables the community to be structured into the form of a thick web of indissoluble links between the subjects who cannot exist or develop outside of it.

[63] György Lukács, *The Ontology of Social Being*, Volume III "Labor," translated by David Fernbach, (London: Merlin Press, 1980), p. 49. Intellectual version of the work division, and outcome, in its own way, of the logic of the "abstract intellect" that breaks down everything, the "academic separateness," the "university compartmentalization" of the knowledge hinders in such a way – which is not at all neutral – every overall view that makes the comprehension of the genesis and the effective configuration of our time possible. Focusing on the single trees makes it, therefore, impossible to have an overview of the forest in its complexity as in its contradictions. The latter, as a fact, never lie in the single parts of the whole, but in the dynamic connections of the parts, in the actuality of the wholeness that hosts them, and that is, thereon, the living "fruit" of their relation.

On the other hand, it is also important to notice how the undoubtedly pragmatic function of Fichte's *The Vocation of the Scholar* neatly surfaces both from the content of Fichte's lectures and their outcomes on the practical level. Part of his audience, as a matter of fact, will create an association with the significative name "League of The Free Men" with the peculiar goal of investigating and spreading the truth about the vocation of man, meant as both a rational and social being and hereafter, of taking action in view of mankind's emancipation. Fichte himself assiduously took part in the meetings of the League, and he was considered a sort of tutelary deity as well as its source of inspiration.

From what we have been saying until now, we should be able to grasp another important point: The translation of *gelehrter* as "scholar," if referring to the theoretical profile sketched out during Fichte's lectures, does not conceal the actual sociopolitical implications of the role. Fichte writes, "Hence, *The Essence of The Scholar* [meant as intellectual], considered as such, is only conceivable in society." It is also the most radical misinterpretation of his spirit, neutralizing *tout court* the most characteristic aspect of Fichte's *The Essence of the Scholar*, that is the symbiotic nexus with his community of belonging.[64] Given that even the most recent tradition kept on translating as scholar Fichte's *gelehrter*, thereon deceiving the spirit of Fichte's thought under the pretext of his letter, it follows that "a gestaltic reorientation" becomes necessary, and this means considering the scholar an intellectual.

In order to shed light on the figure of Fichte's scholar, it can once again be useful to recall Foucault's theoretical elaboration, and in particular some of his considerations in *What is Enlightenment? (Qu'est-ce que les Lumières?*, 1984) about the genesis of the Illuminist critique as instauration of a new form of ontology of actuality (*ontologie de l'actualité*) that analyzes the present time and calls it into question by

---

[64] J.G. Fichte, *The Vocation of the Scholar*, Lecture I: "The Absolute Vocation of Man."

establishing with it a direct and "sagittal relation" without having to compare it, in order to define it, to the previous times.[65] This aspect, blatant for Foucault, especially if we consider Kant's answer to the question *What is Enlightenment?* as implying a "new beginning" for the Western philosophical tradition which, for the first time, employs the historical present as a starting point for his philosophical reflection.

In this sagittal overview of the present time situation, there might lie then the epochal difference in respect to the "analysis of truth" as practised in an exemplary way by Descartes and his research through the *cogito*, namely a universal subject placed—this is the decisive aspect—outside a given historical time.[66]

By following Foucault, with philosophy, critique goes hand in hand with the historical time and becomes a *present time-centered reflection* in a symbiotic nexus with the society wherein the philosopher lives and takes action. This is according to a line which, inaugurated by the Enlightenment (*Aufklärung*), finds its coherent continuation beyond fractures and innovations in Hegel's conception of philosophy, as "its own time comprehended in thoughts" (*ihre Zeit in Gedanken erfaßt*), and in Fichte's understanding of the intellectual as a subject pragmatically acting within the social space of a community.[67] From this perspective, through Foucault's grammar, we could say that if the scholar is the son of the "analysis of the truth," the intellectual originates from a new conception opened up by the ontology of the actuality, and without it, the figure of the intellectual could neither be conceived nor fully understood.

---

[65] M. Foucault, *What is Enlightnement?*, The Foucault Reader, (New York: Pantheon Book, 1984), pp. 32-50.

[66] Immanuel Kant, *An Answer to the Question: What is Enlightenment?*, in *What is Enlightenment, Eighteenth-Century Answers a Twentieth-Century Questions*, ed. and translated by James Schmidt, (London: University of California Press, 1996).

[67] Georg Wilhelm Friedrich Hegel, *Elements of the Philosophy of Right*, ed. by Allen W. Wood, trans. by H.B. Nisbet, (Cambridge: Cambridge University Press, 1991), p. 21.

Foucault's considerations introduce us to the problem of the nexus between the intellectual as meant by Fichte and the intellectual as meant by the Enlightenment. As Hans Georg von Manz has underlined in his essay, *Fichte's Concept of the Scholar in Confrontation with That of the Enlightenment (Fichtes Konzept des Gelehrten in Auseinandersetzung mit demjenigen der Aufklärung)*, Fichte undoubtedly refers, even if in a critical way, to the concept of the scholar as codified by the Enlightenment, especially for what concerns the two interconnected themes of autonomy and sociopragmatic value.[68]

As Fichte outlines, the intellectual is first of all called upon to assert the absolute autonomy of the thought that Kant in his *What is Education?* had summoned in Horatio's motto "have the courage to use your *own* understanding," integrally identifying the Enlightenment with one's courage in making use of one's intelligence. However, this intelligence does not have to be merely theoretical and contemplative, but must be also socially and practically operative and thereon, able to transform the given reality. On this very inheritance from the Enlightenment, Fichte inserts his fiery polemic against the traditional figure of the scholar who, even if the scholar accumulates the treasures of knowledge, egoistically employs it in view of his own cultural self-shaping. It is with the Enlightenment that the scholar becomes the one who thinks of society through society, trying to make a difference in it according to Voltaire's model. Put in Christian Thomasius' formula, philosophy needs to be the instrumental habit to the benefit of the human race (*habitus instrumentalis in utilitatem generis humani*).

Nevertheless, it would be a great mistake to think that the profile of the intellectual as sketched out by Fichte is identical

[68] Hans Georg von Manz, *Fichtes Konzept des Gelehrten in Auseinandersetzung mit demjenigen der Aufklärung*, in C. De Pascale et alii (ed. by), *Fichte und die Aufklärung*, (Hildesheim: Olms, 2004), pp. 285-292.

to the Enlightenment, without which, however, Fichte's profile would not even be thinkable:

> *Fichte's attitude towards the kind of intellectual developed during the Enlightenment is ambivalent. On one side, Fichte agrees with the Enlightenment's criticism of the scholar's inability to transform the world; on the other side, Fichte himself develops an ideal of intellectual that questions the category of the philosopher of the Enlightenment.*[69]

The ideal of *The Essence of the Scholar* outlined by Fichte is in direct contrast with the Enlightenment conception of the intellectual, and in general of the knowledge loose from any tie to the problem of the truth as such (thought of as "founding philosophy"); namely, with the philosophical truth as a science of the wholeness, a wholeness that is ontologically known and axiologically valued, hence Fichte's constant reprimands against the popular philosophy (*Popular-Philosophie*). In other words, Fichte rejects the Enlightenment idea that the intellectual as "ontologist of the actuality," as Foucault would put it, does not have to deal with eternity, with a truth that goes beyond pure utility or perception. With an attitude that characterizes his entire intellectual evolution, Fichte aims for both keeping and overcoming the Enlightenment: He integrally accepts the idea that the philosopher must take action through society, but he also rejects the premise that this would, *de facto*, require the abandonment of the problem of the truth meant as systematic science of the wholeness that is taken away from the abstract intellect's grip.

Fichte's intellectual is then called to deal with society (to act through it and for it) but cannot do so without dealing as well

---

[69] H.G. von Manz, *Fichte's Konzept des Gelehrten in Auseinandersetzung mit demjenigen der Aufklärung*, in C. De Pascale et alii (ed. by), *Fichte und die Aufklärung*, (Hildesheim: Olms, 2004), pp. 285-292. English translation by A. Carnesecchi.

with the metaphysically conceived truth, with the structures that come before the historically determined dimension of society and which make it possible. As for Hegel, and therefore for Fichte, the philosopher in the form of the intellectual must think in his own time and actively act on it. Meanwhile, in order to do it properly, the philosopher (or the intellectual) has to deal with what is always true (in the form of a *philosophical science of the truth)*, especially since, for Fichte no less than for Hegel, in order to think of what is always true, it is necessary to take under examination one's time in a balanced manner, given that what is true does not historically unfold in one's time, but always unfolds in spatiotemporal configurations, namely as becoming-true-of-the-truth, in a genuine monosecular ontology of temporality or, from a different perspective, transcendentally rather than historically, but based on history.

The truth of the becoming-true-of-the-truth process does not exclusively depend upon its unfolding, nor can it be historically annihilated, as truth is placed on the logic-ontological level that preexists its unfolding ("God...is in his eternal essence before the creation of nature and a finite mind," according to a suggestive image of Hegel's *Science of Logic* [*Wissenschaft der Logik]*) in which, no less, it fully unfolds.[70] Truth implies a process of mediation that unfolds over time: In this sense, it remains "true" and, at the same time, becomes historical in the form of a historical monosecular ontology. A large part of the fourth lecture on *The Vocation of the Scholar* will be devoted to this problem, to the indissoluble nexus existing between historical knowledge (one's own time) and philosophical knowledge (what is always true).

Thus, it can be said that the enigma regarding the relation between *Wissenschaftslehre* and *The Vocation of The Intellectual* has been partially solved. Fichte's *The Essence of the Scholar* as well as his own vocation cannot but be thought

---

[70] G.W.F Hegel, *Science of Logic*, (Blackmask Online, 2001) p. 20.

in relation to the ontological truth that determines (*bestimmt*) its configuration. Both the intellectual and his mission—this is the consequence—must be thought of in relation with the *Wissenschaftslehre* that—especially in the third of its principles codified in 1794-1795—focuses on the mission-vocation of the intellectual in accordance with an ontological structure that does not annihilate itself on the sociohistorical level, but instead makes it possible and comprehensible. The very same *Wissenschaftslehre*, for its part, appears as a transposition to the ontological level of the free action (*tathandlung*) of humanity, unitarily conceived of as a unique *Ich* that acts—according to the model of which the intellectual is its champion—in view of its own more and more complete emancipation.

The quick reference to Foucault's distinction between the two conceptions of truth that aporetically co-exist since the Enlightnement's modern era leads this author to give a few more hints, even if in just an impressionistic way, on the figure of the intellectual as he takes shape in direct relation with the ontology of the present. Although it is impossible to be exhaustive, by following Louis Bodin's reconstruction in his *The Intellectual* (*Les intellectual*), the category of the intellectual does not establish itself until the end of the nineteenth century, precisely, on the occasion of the Dreyfus affair—one of the first deplorable public manifestations of mass anti-Semitism that would produce in the following years one of the forms in which evil is manifested on earth—and the consequent Émile Zola's "I Accuse" (*Je accuse*).[71] *The Manifesto of the Intellectuals (Manifeste des intellectuels* which appeared in the "*Aurore*" on January 14th, 1898, represents the genesis of the new word "intellectual." As is well known, the Dreyfus affair—a French official of Jewish descent had been unjustly accused of being a secret agent for the Kaiser of Germany to then be sentenced, degraded, deported to Cayenne, and at the

---

[71] See Louis Bodin, *Les intellectuel*, (Paris: PUF, 1962).

end exonerated and reinstated in the French Army—roused the active intervention of the entire "social estate" of the writers who, guided by Zola, heroically opposed this anti-Semitic campaign through a genuine collective reaction of culture against prejudice.

Since the very beginning, the word "intellectual" refers to a specific social group that employs a specialistic cultural legitimation to assert the worth of a moral, political, and philosophical stance openly enforcing—this is the crucial point—in a social and political way one's own baseline symbolic system. It is also true that in England, the term "intellectual" precociously established itself since about the seventeenth century with a meaning that only minimally corresponded to the expression acquired afterwards and has been used up until the present day. In the rest of Europe, though, the word gained semantic weight after a long time. If we consider that in France, the "intellectual" is still unknown in the 1876 *Littré* dictionary and even in the 1890 dictionary, the entry for "intellectualism" is solely employed as a neologism with a pejorative meaning.

As already briefly said, it was with the Dreyfus affair that the concept of the "intellectual" finds expression in a specific word to which it will remain firmly linked until the current time, not without undergoing some radical transformation in regards to the social function of the intellectuals. In their fight against the anti-Sematic prejudice, since the beginning Dreyfus activists acknowledged themselves as belonging to a specific social group, bearer of an exquisitely social instance, able to impose a radical reconfiguration of culture in the key of a political claim and through social praxis. The fight against prejudice, as a matter of fact, was taken up by a group that was self-aware. Aware of its role, the latter took political action in the name of its own culture, the knowledge of which it was the standard-bearer. This group of intellectuals, far from being confined in the hyperuranic sky of theory, had its actual sociopolitical worth in an effective (and claimed) incident on the structures of power and on the system of the existing society.

From a different perspective, the group employed a specialistic social legitimization in order to assert the validity of a committed stance on the political, moral, and philosophical level aimed at potentially transforming the system in view of its accordance with the principles it claimed.[72] Thus, culture became practical energy, a weapon of political struggle, an expression of the refusal of a society not yet configured according to the principles of reason.

As highlighted by Costanzo Preve, the term "intellectual" is characterized on the one hand for its quite recent origin and its specific and exclusive semantic field, and on the other hand for its irresistible attraction towards the meta-historical universalization. On this universal basis, according to the logic of the "risky category of the path"—or *percorrimento* as Foucault used to call it—the category of the intellectual ends up enclosing in a totally paradoxical way the figures most far apart on this path from Egyptian priests to Athenian sophists, from the Dominican monks to the seventeenth century philosophes.[73]

That this deeply ambiguous status of the word is suspended between a particular genesis and universal validity is not surprising: As we have seen, if it is true that the word has a specific date of birth, the figure of the intellectual is contemporary to the genesis of the Illuminist ontology of the actuality. Thus, it is understandable that there is an apparent paradox of coexistence in the same linguistic unit of opposite meanings. Fichte calls the scholar the subject that, by fully coinciding with the modern figure of the intellectual, represents the overturning of the scholar in traditional sense,

---

[72] See Costanzo Preve, *Il ritorno del clero. La questione degli intellettuali oggi*, (C.R.T.: Pistoia, 1999), p. 5. For what concerns the time in which we live in, Preve distinguishes between "secular clergy" (the media) and "regular clergy" (the universities which give legitimacy to the world order), both they have in common the symbolic-religious doubling of the capitalistic asset.

[73] See ibid., p. 38 on.

namely the profile that the German area of tradition had solely defined as a scholar. Anyway, it would be simplistic to describe the modern conception of the intellectual in a monolithic form (regardless of his specific plural actualizations) and unilaterally insist upon relevant isomorphisms which, beyond the differences, are to a certain extent the common basis to the proliferation of the heterogeneous figure of the intellectual during the modern era, both before and after the Dreyfus affair.

In a nutshell, by significantly simplifying the matter, there are two big possibilities in which to conceive and practice the role of the intellectual: On the one hand, the particular way the figure of the "organic intellectual" is codified in an exemplary fashion by Antonio Gramsci, and on the other hand, finding in Fichte his champion, states a universalistic principle. On one side is an acknowledgement of the relative autonomy of the intellectual production as such, and on the other side, takes as its own destination the universality of mankind's emancipation (not the particularity of a social class, estate, nation, etc.).[74]

If the line of interpretation that refers to Gramsci directly links the category of the intellectuals to one of the two major social estates in the agonistic ground of the civil society by considering the intellectual "organic," either to the bourgeoisie or to the proletariat, there is no third option (*tertium non datur*). Fichte's standpoint, in its own way heir to the era of Enlightenment, is instead predominantly universalistic, conceiving the intellectual as organic to the truth and therefore, to mankind transcendentally meant as a "singular-collective" subject. In accordance with this macro-distinction, if Gramsci's intellectual is organic to the part, Fichte's intellectual is organic to the whole, and according to Husserl's fitting formula is "humanity's officer" (or, if you like, to mankind conceived as a whole), regardless of the distinctions,

---

[74] See G. Mantovani, *Gramsci: l'intellettuale organico*, in "Vita e pensiero," n. 2, XLIX, February 1996, pp. 173-183.

fragmentations, and stratifications in which it is actualized. With Husserl's own words in his *Crisis* (*Krisis*):

> *We are indeed what we are, as we are the officers of the modern philosophical humanity, the heirs and the bearers of that orientation of the will that crosses it. And we are so on the basis of an original foundation that is, at the same time, a re-foundation and transformation of the original Greek foundation.*[75]

In this way, it follows that we have what Karl Mannheim defined as "intellectuality free from ties" (*freischwebende Intelligenz*), ties that are nothing but those with truth, or better, with the free search of it.[76] Without dwelling here on the multiple shades of these two big categories and on the different possible permutations of them, inside each of them are permutations that would, actually, lead to a number—not small indeed—of sub-classifications. This author presents these here as a significative possible mediation between the two, the solution outlined and practised by Jean-Paul Sartre— the Voltaire of the French Left—through the figure of the *intellectuel engagé*.[77] The "engaged intellectual" à la Sartre

---

[75] Edmund Husserl, *Die Krisis der europäischen Wissenschaften und die transzendentale Phänomenologie. Eine Einleitung in die phänomenologische Philosophie*, 1936 (1950); tr. it. ed. by W. Biemel, *La crisi delle scienze europee e la fenomenologia trascendentale: introduzione alla filosofia fenomenologica*, (Milan: Il Saggiatore, 1983), p. 99. See C. Pacchiani, *L'idea della scienza in Husserl*, (Padoa: CEDAM, 1973). On the theoretical nexus between Fichte and Husserl, see H. Tietjen, Fichte und Husserl: *Letztbegründung, Subjektivität und praktische Vernunft im transzendentalen Idealismus*, (Frankfurt: Klostermann, 1980).

[76] See K. Mannheim, *Ideologie und Utopie*, 1929; tr. it. *Ideologia e utopia*, (Bologna: II Mulino, 1985). For a reading of Mannheim's concept of "intelligence free from ties," see A. Neusüss, *Utopisches Bewusstsein und freischwebende Intelligenz. Zur Wissenssoziologie Karl Mannheims*, (Maisenheim am Glan: Hain, 1968).

[77] On the figure of the "engaged intellectual" outlined by Sartre, see the following works: P. Naville, *L'intellectuel communiste: à propos de Jean-Paul Sartre*, (Paris: Rivière, 1956); A. Mancarella, *L'intellettuale e il potere: saggio su Sartre*, (Manduria: Lacaita, 1977); P. Sosso, *Chierico, artista, intellettuale: la funzione dell'homme de lettres da Benda a Sartre*, (Turin: Théleme, 2004);

keeps the distance from the abyss—Gramsci's organicity—in which he could fall, and maintains his autonomy of thought, his own "freedom from ties," if we recall Mannheim's significant formula. [78] In this sense, the *intellectuel engagé* certainly engages himself, taking even radical stances, but maintaining his own freedom of thought, giving and revoking his adhesion to social and political causes, case to case, rationally motivating from time to time the reason for which he joins or dissociates himself from the group and party line to which he feels closer, although he never adheres to it in a definite and irrevocable form. He is, first of all, organic to the truth and in the name of this organicity, given different contexts, adheres or dissociates himself from groups, parties, and social classes, according to the way they relate with the universal principle of reference.

It has been mentioned that Sartre's solution, because it is the only one that allows us to clarify an aspect of the organic intellectual once it has been understood, permits one to decipher in a more precise form the essence of Fichte's universalistic scholar and, at the same time, its preferability compared to any other possible model. The fact that the committed intellectual (*intelectiuel engage*) is engaged without irrevocably adhering to any specific group—maintaining, therefore, as a matter of fact, his exclusive organicity to the truth—highlights in the most evident way what is actually the principal limit of the organicity as meant by Gramsci. As suggested by Preve, in Gramsci's model there is a dangerous slipping towards the "absolute sociologism" that, because it is relativist and nihilist by nature, considers social class, group, and party as the only ethical criterion of good and evil. [79] Instead of being master or educator, according to Fichte's view,

---

A. Boschetti, *L'impresa intellettuale: Sartre e "Les temps modernes,"* (Bari: Dedalo 1984).

[78] Upon the figure of the "disorganic intellectual," with particular attention to the Frankfurt School, see L. Geninazzi, *Horkheimer & C. Gli intellettuali disorganici,* (Milan: Jaca Book, 1976).

[79] See C. Preve, *Il ritorno del clero. La questione degli intellettuali oggi,* p. 38

the intellectual is, in such a way, devalued as mere producer of ideological frameworks at the service of a group of reference, in a forced convergence of what is true and what is functional to the group.

From this point of view, the organic intellectual inevitably falls victim of the "identity block," which is the neutralization of his own role of "free intelligence" called to show the way to the group in view of what is true. His role is then reduced to the (purely ideological and devoid of any truth-oriented instance) one of a hetero-directed pawn that must employ his intelligence to demonstrate the coincidence of the truth with what the group establishes, or with what is, anyway, convenient for the latter. It is a relativistic sociologism because the truth depends upon what is functional to the survival, the empowerment, and the hegemony of one side, by unconditionally liquidating as false everything that opposes it. Thus, the "identity block" makes impossible any identity innovation that may become incompatible with the tetragon presupposed by the group organicity. In this way, theoretical activity and thought—far from being free in view of a critical search for the truth and practice the following unmasking of falsity and ideologies (maybe by criticising the actions of the group itself)—are aprioristically bound to maintaining organicity, identity, and the inescapable membership to a sociological group of reference. This happens because—it is better to insist—the fact that whatever theory or thought may be elaborated and assumed as a untranscendable precondition, it will have a validity only if organic and therefore functional to the survival and reproduction of a group.

The physiological weakness of such a perspective is blatant: On the one hand, theoretical activity is claimed to be valid only if, as its prerequisite, it guarantees organicity to the part (social class, party or group), and on the other hand, the outcomes of such activity are consolidated afterwards and only if considered compatible with the initial assumption.[80] In this sense, as Preve clarified, organicity has a specific circular structure by positing *a priori* what must be demonstrated afterwards, and therefore, reducing the intellectual activity to a mere theoretical legitimization of the group's choices.[81] Not only is the truthful space of the philosophical activity in this way neutralized under the blows of nihilistic sociologism, but is also reduces to zero the *a priori* possibility of "epistemological ruptures" (Gaston Bachelard) and of "scientific revolution" (Thomas Kuhn). Any innovator who dares to discover something that is not compatible with the alleged organicity is automatically expelled from the identity community as traitor, renegade, repentant, etc., no matter what are his actual discoveries. [82] The group cannot be renewed, amended, or improved through the philosophical truth, as the latter is neutralized under the blows of the relativist sociologism. The numerous identity tribes of nineteenth century Marxism offer an unsurpassed example of this organistic logic, enemy of any universal principle of reference.

As Preve suggested, Gramsci's organicity makes impossible any development or scientific progress, inasmuch as the essential prerequisite for advancement in the theoretical field consists in the possibility of freely arriving at theses that eventually imply an exodus from the posited organicity and from the identity block.[83] Once again, by taking off the outer layers of Fichte's guide for mankind, the intellectual is reduced to being one of a group of theoretical justifiers on the ideological level. Consequently, his activity is reduced to a harmless and sterile identity fable, exclusively finalized to ideologically confirm once more his membership in a group which, according to that form that Louis Althusser has iconoclastically summed

---

[80] See ibid., 23 on.
[81] Ibid., p. 39.
[82] See ibid., pp. 40 on.
[83] See ibid., pp. 37-38.

up in the expression "telling each other stories"(*se raconter d'histoires*)."

Thanks to this detour which made us focus, even though with quick references, on the intellectual engagement (*engage*) outlined by Sartre, the differences should be clearer by now between the organic intellectual *à la* Gramsci and the universalistic intellectual *à la* Fichte, and the preferability of the latter. The first one passively joins the group and does nothing but intellectually work through the symbolic mediation for the reproduction of the group. Instead, the second is organic uniquely to the free search for the truth and only in a second moment—without ever renouncing his own universalistic organicity—identifies with a group which in actual context is the bearer of a universalistic stance. The first one is entirely functional to the group and its survival; the second freely joins a specific group whenever the algorithm that translates the particular into the universal is seen: Namely a claim universally oriented towards the emancipation of mankind, transcendentally meant—according to Fichte's grammar—as *I*, as the only acting subject.

As Fichte upholds in the first lecture on the intellectual (1794), "all the powers of man, which are essentially but one power, had only become distinguished in their application to different objects, should all accord in perfect unity and harmony with each other."[84] This is, by the way, the secret opening key to understanding the expressive unitary function of Fichte's thought as "proposer of philosophical knowledge characterized by both rigorous critical spirit and founding tension." His pervicacious underlying philosophical code is always there, despite all of the turns, innovations, and paradigmatic changes that characterize Fichte's intellectual journey (*Denkweg*).[85]

Animated by the universal organicity, Fichte's conceptual constellation is permanently crossed by his search for universal

---

[84] J.G. Fichte, *The Vocation of the Scholar*, Lecture I.
[85] Marco Ivaldo, *Fichte: l'assoluto e l'immagine*, (Rome: Studium, 1983), p. 11.

emancipation made possible by the particulars that can be found either in the intellectual class in *The Vocation of the Scholar*, in *The Closed Commercial State*, in the *Speeches to the German Nation*, or in the religious community in *The Way Towards the Blessed Life*. In this sense, in opposition to what is commonplace and prejudicial, the intellectual as conceived by Marx is—in a Fichtian way—organic to the truth coinciding with the exposition of the falsity of the whole (namely of the society capitalistically structured).[86] Only in a second moment does this adhere to that particular group—the proletariat—in order to defend its own particular interest (the liberation from the "radical chains" that weigh on him), and claims the universal emancipation (the transcendental overcoming of the capitalistic cosmos as a precondition of the universal emancipation of mankind).[87]

Fichte, in his codification of the scholar as a social figure, counterposed retrospectively to the traditional scholar as well as prospectively to the organic intellectual, asserts a radical critique of the postmodern intellectual class that integrally adheres to the logic of the power—a real catastrophic parable of the scholar's mission.[88] The intellectuals' transition towards the reproduction of the crystallization of power through an elaborate ideological framework marks the climax of, as Zygmunt Bauman called it, the "decaying process of the

---

[86]See Theodor Ludwig Wiesengrund Adorno, *Minima Moralia. Reflexionen aus dem beschädigten Leben*, 1951; tr. it. ed. by R. Solmi, *Minima moralia. Meditazioni della vita offesc*, (Turin: Einaudi 1979), p. 48: "il tutto è falso" (*das Ganze ist das Unwahre*). On the implications of the "negative dialectic" activated by the assumptions of the falsity of the whole in Adorno's thought, see also M. Vacatello, *Th.W. Adorno. Il rinvio della prassi*, (Florence: La Nuova Italia, 1972).

[87] On Marx's universalistic perspective, see especially Preve, *Marx inattuale. Eredità e prospettiva*, (Turin: Bollati Boringhieri, 2004). This author also refers to his *Bentornato Marx! Rinascita di un pensiero rivoluzionario* (Milan: Bompiani, 2009) and *Karl Marx e la schiavitù salariata: uno studio sul lato cattivo della storia* (Padoa: Il Prato, 2007).

[88] On this point the author refers to his *Minima mercatalia. Filosofia e capitalismo*, (Milan: Bompiani, 2012), with A. Tagliapietra's introductive essay, pp. 376.

intellectuals." Such process provoked the fall of the intellectuals from the original role of "community legislators" (indeed, in this lies the secret of Fichte's *Vocation of the Scholar*) to the role of unresponsive interpreters and passive witnesses to a sociopolitical world, which must not be obviously modified in the course of overturning the duty programmatically assigned by Fichte to the intellectual class.[89]

Against the intellectuals' integral adherence to the logic of power and to the sanctifying reproduction of the system—genuine fulfillment of the adaptation (*Anpassung)* of the world order—Fichte's stance in his *Vocation of the Scholar* is effectively the most extraordinary description of the universalistic-emancipatory role of the intellectual. In the form of a commitment universally led, the goal of the intellectual is directly related to the idea of humanity and mankind's emancipation through the transforming praxis according to that social and collective effort always undertaken from scratch, and aimed at the full and harmonious agreement between the *I* and *not-I*. Between humanity and its actual social objectivations, the intellectual takes action in view of a complete uniformity with the ontologic possibility mankind has always postponed until tomorrow. Fichte's intellectual, guided by the idea that "reality should be judged starting from ideals and modified (*modificirt)* by those who are believed to be capable of," is called to undertake the role of "teacher of the human race" (*Lehrer des Menschengeschlechtes*) as a guide for mankind towards emancipation and withal, a stubborn refusal to accept the existing reality as a "given fact," independent from human activity, and thereon, unable to be transcended.[90]

It is noteworthy that, in the lectures on *The Vocation of the Scholar* while outlining the duty of the intellectual, Fichte

---

[89] See Zygmunt Bauman, *Legislators and Interpreters. On Modernity, Post-Modernity and Intellectuals*, (Polity Press: 1987). On the genesis of the figure of the intellectual see L. Bodin, *Les intellectuel*, pp. 68 ss. See also E.W. Said, *Representations of the Intellectual*, 1994, edited and translated by M. Gregorio, *Dire la verità. Gli intellettuali e il potere*, (Milan: Feltrinelli, 1995)
[90] J.G. Fichte, *The Vocation of the Scholar*. Lecture I.

expressively introduces such a figure as one who has to induce humanity to acquire through culture the consciousness of his destination, codified according to the principles of *Wissenschaftslehre* as an unexhausted (because never ending) process of conformation of actuality to human subjectivity and of conformation of the latter to its ontological possibilities:

> *If the Ego is to be constantly at one with itself in this respect also, it must strive to operate directly upon the things themselves on which the sensations and perceptions of man depend; man must endeavour to modify these, and to bring them into harmony with the pure form of his Ego, so that his conceptions on them likewise, so far as these (his conceptions) depend upon the nature of their objects, may harmonize with that form.* [91]

We could possibly claim that within Fichte's lectures beats the heart of the project towards mankind's emancipation, the unfolding of which is essential for the transformation of the scholar to intellectual through acquiring a consciousness of the actuality of humanity's duties for the future: First, freedom as a never ending process of liberation from the present time difficulties and from the contradictions that lie in its most intimate structures.

This is exemplified in *Pereira Maintains* by Antonio Tabucchi, wherein the protagonist gradually develops the consciousness of his specific social role in the process of achievement of freedom against the objectivations that interpose with its unfolding. *Pereira Maintains* is a real novel of education that tells the story of the gradual transformation of the scholar into intellectual. Likewise, Fichte's scholar is called to leave the initial duty of the scholar to acquire the intellectual's one, which is appositive and organic to the universal goal of human emancipation. [92]

---

[91] Ibid.
[92] See Antonio Tabucchi, *Sostiene Pereira*, (Milan: Feltrinelli, 1994).

It follows that in Fichte's text, we can find the most splendid description of the intellectual "free from ties" (Mannheim), "officer of the humanity" (Husserl) and never "organic" (Gramsci) to a group, but on a case-by-case basis "engaged" (Sartre) according to his free thought, just when his group may, through the defence of its own particularism, promote for this very reason, universal emancipation.

The most surprising anticipation of this vocation can be found, even though just sketched and not fully developed, in Spinoza's inorganic, inhomogeneous, and misaligned stance if compared to the seventeenth century Dutch production. By keeping a distance from any direct or indirect apologetics of his own historical world, Spinoza bravely demonstrated his "inorganic" approach with respect to his own social cosmos through the codification of the philosophy of freedom (*libertas philosophandi*), his expulsion in July 1656 from the Jewish community, and his refusal of the prestigious chair at the University of Heidelberg. In such a way, he remained—for Fichte—a free intellectual who had nothing to do with any form of ideological involvement, but exclusively engaged in the process of human emancipation. [93] We could say that, like Fichte, Spinoza does not reject the commitment, and his entire theoretical elaboration is nothing more than a great attempt to demonstrate *more geometrico* the ontological and political

---

[93] The letter, dated March 30th, 1673 – in B. Spinoza, *Tutte le opere*, ed. by A. Sangiacomo, (Milan: Bompiani, 2010), pp. 2067-2069 – is itself a heroic claim of autonomy of the thought. "Since I have never had the intention to teach publically, I cannot take advantage of this splendid occasion, for how much I have been pondering on it. As a fact, in the first place I think that if I had to deal with the education of the young people, I would have to cease to promote philosophy. Furthermore, I think I do not know the limits in which this freedom of doing philosophy (*libertas philosophandi*) must be enclosed in order not to look like I want to perturb the religion that is publically stated. Hence, my illustrious Lord, you may see that my reluctance does not depend upon the hope of a better luck, but upon the love I have for tranquillity (*tranquillitatis amoris*) that I believe achievable if I abstain from public teaching." English translation by A. Carnesecchi. See A. Tosel, *Du materialisme de Spinoza*, (Paris: Kime, 1994); R. Ciccarelli, *Immanenza e politica in Spinoza*, (Rome: Aracne, 2006).

necessity of a "democratic communitarianism."[94] This is according to the belief—expressed in his Ethics (*Ethica*) in a language that combines ontological, ethical, and political determinations—that the ontological unity of the substance shall be reflected in the sociopolitical dimension, as a communitarian unity that coexists with the kaleidoscopic free proliferation of the differences.[95]

Fichte's universalistic vocation anticipated by Spinoza will later be recalled by Edmund Husserl who, as noted above, not only will outline in a Fichtian way the intellectuals' duty as the "officers of humanity" (*Funktionare der Menschheit*), but also will devote his lectures to "Fichte's ideal of humanity" (*Fichtes Menscheitsideal*) between November 8th and November 17th, 1917, at the Faculty of Political Science of the University of Freiburg in front of an audience of soldiers following the day of the Russian Revolution. Then in the following year, Husserl will reuse the former lectures for the students of the Faculty of Philosophy.[96] From Husserl's point of view, the most surprising aspect of Fichte's codification of the role of the human being and of the intellectual (with Fichte defined as "an ethical-religious reformer, mankind's educator, prophet, and seer")[97] as "the new shape that he gave to the ideals of an authentic humanity starting from the deepest springs of his philosophy,"

---

[94] On this point, see the following works: A. Deregibus, *La filosofia etico-politica di Spinoza*, (Turin: Giappichelli, 1963); A. Campanale, *Diritto e politica tra necessità e libertà nel pensiero di Spinoza*, (Pisa: ETS, 1993); S. Zac, *Philosophie, théologie, politique dans l'œuvre de Spinoza*, (Paris: Vrin, 1979); L. Mugnier-Pollet, *La philosophie politique de Spinoza*, (Paris: Vrin, 1976); A. Tosel, *Spinoza ou le crépuscule de la servitude. Essai sur le Traité Théologico-politique*, (Paris: Aubier, 1984); M. Chaui *Spinoza e la politica*, (Milan: Ghibli, 2005).

[95] On the nexus between individual and community, see A. Matheron, *Individu et communauté chez Spinoza*, (Paris: Minuit, 1988). Per quel che, invece, riguarda la relazione tra politica e affetti, see F. Bonicalzi, *L'"impensato della politica. Spinoza e il vincolo civile*, (Naples: Guida, 1999).

[96] See E. Husserl, *Fichte e l'ideale di umanità: tre lezioni*, ed. by F. Rocci, (Pisa: ETS, 2006). See. J.G. Hart, *Husserl and Fichte. With Special Regard to Husserl's Lectures on "Fichte's Ideal of Humanity,"* in "Husserl Studies," n. 12 (1995), pp. 135-163.

[97] Ibid., English translation by A. Carnesecchi.

in coherence with the principle of the *Wissenschaftslehre* that, as we have seen before, makes of *The Vocation of the Scholar* the specification from the perspective of society (*sub specie communitatis*) of Fichte's theoretical structure. [98] "All his ethical religious intentions—specifies Husserl—have in Fichte a "theoretical anchoring" which in the end, refers to the structure of *Wissenschaftslehre* as a foundation (*fundamentum*) of theory as well as praxis, given the inextricable unity between Fichte's two codifications. Hereafter, we will focus on this point.[99]

---

[98] Ibid., p. 50
[99] Ibid., p. 51.

◆

We may therefore say that mutual improvement—improvement of ourselves by the freely admitted action of others upon us, and improvement of others by our reaction upon them as upon free beings—is our vocation in Society.

J.G. Fichte, *The Vocation of the Scholar*, Lecture II

◆

In one word, through the adoption and general spreading of the *Science of Knowledge* amongst those for whom it is written, the whole human race will have been rid of the rule of blind chance, and fate will have been annihilated. Mankind will henceforth control itself under the rule of its own conception, and will henceforth make out of itself with absolute freedom all that can be made out of it.

J.G. Fichte, *A Sun-Clear Statement*

◆

3.

The Doctrine of Knowledge as Fundamentum of the Lectures on the Intellectual

◆

According to the assumption which has been explicitly expressed from the beginning, and which we are going to examine more expansively, in the 1794 lectures on *The Vocation of the* Scholar there is a constant referral to the ontology of praxis upon which is based the 1794-1795 *The Science of the Right (Fundamental Principles of the Whole Doctrine of Knowledge)*. The lectures are a coherent development of the actual sociopolitical dimension configured as the consequent articulation of the third principle of the *Wissenschaftslehre* ("I counterpose, in the *I*, to a divisible *I*, a divisible *not-I*").[100]

In the following pages, Fichte's lectures will be retraced with a three-fold objective: (a) To present a synoptic bird's-eye view, focusing on the most relevant turning points. (b) To

---

[100] Ibid., p. 181. English translation by A. Carnesecchi.

demonstrate once more their symbiotic nexus with the *Wissenschaftslehre* in the attempt of (c) Highlighting how the latter may find in them a coherent sociopolitical development. This will allow us to clarify the continuity and the existing symmetry of the references between the 1794 lectures and the 1794-1795 *Wissenschaftslehre*.

Before going into the analysis of the contents of each lecture, it is good to make a few more general considerations upon their structure, as well as the theoretical system upon which they are based. In general terms, the foundation of the *Lectures on The Scholar's Vocation* is the inseparable nexus between freedom and action (according to the hendiadys of "free action"). The foundation of Fichte's system is given in the form of an identity for which freedom is the transformative action and unconditional standpoint in overcoming objectivations. "*I*" is essentially unconditional freedom, and it is so because it is not a positive *something*, but a Sisyphean *action*, not *being*: An unceasing *unfolding* (the concept of Spirit as "pure action" by Gentile—Fichte *redivivus*—is herein entirely enclosed), an unexhausted opus of transcending the existing reality in his concrete historical crystallizations.[101]

Because it is the result of *I*'s praxis, the same "*not-I*" exists as something known and believed to be true (*Tatsache*)—as a "result of the action" and not as a stand-alone "autonomous thing" (*Ding an sich*). This coincides with the set of particular and contingent items, namely the objectivations put in place by the subject that are like this. However, they could be otherwise eventually, depending on the praxis that put them in place and which, according to moral necessity, can equally and must always take them away again. It is from a rigorously practical perspective that, on the other hand, the question which otherwise would be irremediably unsolved finds its answer: Why does the *I* put in place the *not-I*? This question could also

---

[101] On this topic, see H.S. Harris, *Fichte e Gentile*, in "Giornale critico della filosofia italiana," 1964, pp. 557-578.

be put in the form of a more cogent dilemma, such as why is the *being* meant as resistance against acting subjectivity?

As is well-known, from Fichte's point of view, the *I* posits the *not-I* in order to limit itself, to set an obstacle to overcome, namely to exercise the praxis that unceasingly is. It is only by acting that the *I* realizes itself, and in order to act, it needs an object to stand against (*Gegenstant*) upon which to exercises its action. Freedom, on the other hand, would never acquire self-consciousness and put in place any action if it did not meet an obstacle, a resistance (*Widerstand*): The concrete action is always given in the form of a hindered action, so that the *not-I* "absolutely is, thanks to *I*'s action, and for no any other reason." [102] In harmony with this praxis structure, on September 12th, 1798, in one of his letters, Fichte wrote a crucial passage which better than any other, reveals the spirit of his philosophy: "I would like to do something, as much as possible, through spoken and written word: This is my life's goal; for how better is the field of action, better I feel."[103]

From what has been claimed, it follows that if the *not-I* were not given, then the very same *I* could not exist as transforming praxis, as an insuppressible effort to transcend the hindering objectualities that generate its praxis. It is then, in its always-reiterated clash (*Anstoß*) against the *not-I*, that the *I* can exist as praxis, namely according to its most peculiar essence. By following the turns of Fichte's reasoning to the *I* in its being towards the infinite, an obstacle *happens* to slow down the unlimited activity making it a determined activity instead. The obstacle may happen, but at the same time this very obstacle needs to be meant as self-standing, namely as objectivity separated from the subjectivity and opposed to it. Otherwise, it would not be a resistance or hindrance, but a mere duplicate of the positing subject. In other terms, if there were not an obstacle, if the *I* were not limited, it would not have the activity

[102] J.G. Fichte, *Werke. Auswahl in sechs Bänden*, ed. by F. Medicus, 1920-1925, second edition, I, p. 266. English translation by A. Carnesecchi.
[103] Id., *Briefwechsel*, I, p. 593. English translation by A. Carnesecchi.

(*Tätigkeit*) or ability to self-impose with no end; namely, it would fall into that inertia that is the negation of the *I* as limitless praxis, because it is always renewable.[104] Laziness, cowardice, and sloth are consequently the three most serious faults of which humanity and each human being could be held accountable. As Bernard Bourgeois underlined, for Fichte "the moral evil, therefore, consists in the lazy ceasing of the effort of whatever pleasure or indifference may be."[105] In his words from 1794-1795:[106]

> *If* I's *activity did not proceed infinitively (ins Unendliche), the* I *could not limit its activity, could not establish for it any border, as anyway it has too.* I's *activity consists in the unlimited unfolding of itself; against it there is a resistance. If it gave up to this resistance (Widerstand), then that activity that goes beyond the border of the resistance would be completely annihilated and suppressed.*[107]

In this sense, the *not-I* corresponds to the self-alienation that happens to the *I*-Narcissus, when he cannot recognize himself in the water's reflection—counterposing a "nature," an "objectivity" as an object upon which he will exert his own action. The latter is refractory obscurity and at the same time intimate familiarity, depending integrally upon the self-asserting activity of the *I*, and at the same time, it is apparently independent and autonomous. It is indeed to highlight the absolute dependency of the objective world from the acting subjectivity (thought of as a unique subject) that

---

[104] On this aspect, see A. Philonenko, *Théorie et Praxis dans la pensée morale et politique de Kant et de Fichte en 1793*, (Paris: Vrin, 1968), pp. 46 ss.

[105] Bernard Bourgeois, *L'idéalisme de Fichte*, (Paris: PUF, 1968), p. 91. English translation by A. Carnesecchi.

[106] See W. Class & co, *Kommentar zu Fichtes "Grundlage der gesamten Wissenschaftslehre,"* (Amsterdam: Rodopi, 2004).

[107] J.G. Fichte, *Grundlage der gesamten Wissenschaftslehre*, 1795; Italian translation ed. by. G. Boffi, *Fondamento dell'intera dottrina della scienza*, (Milan: Bompiani, 2003), pp. 403-405. English translation by A. Carnesecchi.

Fichte chose the apparently dubious and slippery expression "*not-I.*"

> *The expression* "not-I" *that had raised right away [Fichte's] contemporaries' mockery and did not have a great fortune...conveys a series of meanings. Beside the "object," indicates the "matter," namely what is "given" in one's perception, the "thing," or the "being," as separated from the subject, or even the past of the* I *compared to its actual present. But these specific meanings are not as much important as the theoretical role of this figure as "opposed" (Gegenteil) to the* I. *By coining this expression, Fichte wanted to reiterate that what is perceived and thought is knowable only because there is a subject and through the laws of the latter. The* not-I *is, therefore, conditioned by the* I.[108]

It could be also said that, in accordance with Fichte's argumentative lines, to give a limit means also to assert oneself as limited, as a means for the *I* to assert itself as the "*not*" of its own infinite self-asserting, or better, infinitely reiterated. In this sense, the *not-I* is once more functional to the very same *I*, as the latter (thanks to the *I* clashing against the *not-I*) is limited and slowed down, thus resulting in being determined. In this way, it is posited that the effort (*Streben*) which infinitely aims at assertion of itself as identical to every object will lead the *not-I* to the *I*, by which means always removing the very *not-I*, because "an activity that goes beyond the object becomes an effort by actually going beyond (overcoming) the object," [109] according to the principle of the primacy of the practical reason (*Praktische Vernunft*) that is the *basso*

---

[108] C. Cesa, *Introduzione a Fichte*, p. 19. English translation by A. Carnesecchi.
[109] J.G. Fichte, *Fondamento dell'intera dottrina della scienza*, p. 527. English translation by A. Carnesecchi.

continuo of the *Some Lectures on the Scholar*:[110] "Act (*handeln*)! Act!—It is to that end that we are here."[111]

In *The Science of the Right*, the *I* is at the same time asserting itself and self-counterposing.[112] It follows that *I* (or also "selfhood" [*Ichheit*]) and *not-I* are not realities that are given in different ontological fields like the two *res* by Descartes of the physical world and the mind or consciousness (*res cogitans* and *res extensa*). On the contrary, *I* and *not-I* exist in a tensional and dialectical relation, in which the one asserts the other and always and again tries to remove it in order to assert itself. By following the turns of *The Science of the Right*, *I* and *not-I* come to a conflict in an essential way, in an opposition that cannot ever be completely removed unless it is on a lower level, namely like a limited divisible opposition in relation with the finite level of the human world. The third principle of the *Wissenschaftslehre* claims that: "I counterpose, in the *I*, to the divisible *I*, a divisible *not-I*" (*Ich setze im Ich dem teilbaren Ich ein teilbares Nicht-Ich entgegen*).[113]

In other words, for Fichte the absolute conflict is resolvable only by assuming another unconditioned action (not in the form but in the content) on a different level from the very pure formal unconditionality of the two principles of the *Wissenschaftslehre*. It is what happens with the third principle of *Wissenschaftslehre* that allows the opposition, which cannot be overcome on the absolute level and only removed on a different and lower level. The synthesis can be given only by

---

[110] "It is not the theoretical faculty to make possible the practice, but on the contrary, only the practical faculty makes possible the theoretical one. In itself, Reason is merely practical and becomes theoretical only by applying its laws to a *not-I* that limits it." (Id., Werke. Auswahl in sechs Bänden, cit., I, p. 321). English translation by A. Carnesecchi.

[111] J.G. Fichte, *The Vocation of the Scholar*, Lecture V. Unlike what Philonenko has upheld, this author believes that Fichte's practical instance comes from Kant only. See Philonenko, *Téorie et praxis dans la pensée morale et politique de Kant et de Fichte en 1793*; Id., *Métaphysique et politique chez Kant et Fichte*, (Paris: Vrin, 1997). Fichte's praxis is always social, linked to the community and not to a single individual who is solipsistically considered.

[112] See J.G. Fichte, *Fondamento dell'intera dottrina della scienza*, p. 177.

[113] Ibid., p. 181.

deferring the contradiction on a real quantitative level, by entrusting it to the "quantity capability" (*Quantitatsfähigkeit*) and to the reciprocal determination of *I* and *not-I*. The *I* and *not-I*, since they are absolutely opposed, determine the third principle's goal, and they structure as well an *infinite duty*.[114] Therefore, the asymptotic effort of enhancement through action is founded and, at the same time, the mission of the intellectual as mankind's guide by means of culture is in the process of getting closer to the full correspondence of humanity with itself.

With the third principle, then, is established the relation between two principles that could absolutely not be together (*I* and *not-I*). "How can they be thought together, without them to annihilate and suppress each other, positive A and negative A, to be and not to be, reality and negation?... They limit each other."[115] The goal set up by the third principle is to put in place the relation in which the object that is always the subjective (*Gengenstand*) and never the objective (*Objekt*), namely the result of the positionality of the *I* itself and never existing regardless of the thetic act (the *I* does not exist without its negation). It is not a coincidence that Fichte also calls it "against the part" (*Gegen-Teil*) to underline the conditional existence of the *I*—as it may correlate and participate with the subjective without absolute opposition bringing them to their mutual destruction and elimination.[116] The contradiction is not removed and not removable on the absolute level. It is removed as a limited divisible opposition in relation to the dimension of the finite, as the third principle of science actually proclaims: "I counterpose, in the *I*, to the divisible *I* a divisible *not-I*."[117] In this way—it is good to insist on this matter because herein lies

---

[114] About the way Fichte's philosophy of history's cardinal points come from the *Doctrine of Science's* assumptions, see G.V. Di Tommaso, *Dottrina della scienza e genesi della filosofia della storia nel primo Fichte*, (L'Aquila: Japadre, 1986).
[115] J.G. Fichte, *Fondamento dell'intera dottrina della scienza*, p. 177. English translation by A. Carnesecchi.
[116] Ibid., p. 497-499.
[117] Ibid., p. 81.

the secret to decipher the symbiotic nexus between the *Vocation of the Scholar* and the *Wissenschaftslehre*—the human's duty of action together with its endlessness in "always starting over again" are founded.

As demonstrated by Philonenko, the relation between *I* and *not-I* is integrally enclosed in the third category, the one of the relation which is coessential to the third principle of *The Science of the Right*. [118] This category consists in that "reciprocal action" (*Wechselwirkung*) implying the concrete action in the historical dimension upon the "things" (transforming them in view of their conformity to the *Ichneit*[119]), but also upon the other finite rational beings, in view of a general harmony that, in one respect, may make possible mankind's unity through the effort of each of its members. It is indeed in this work of action upon the others that Fichte founds the mission of the intellectual in society, in the form of "giving" and "receiving"—it is in this way the reciprocal *I* and *not-I* interact in the third principle of the *Foundations of Natural Right* which results in the sociopolitical level of *The Vocation of the Scholar*.

The third principle, by asserting the "divisibility" of the *I* and *not-I*, allows that both the *I* and *not-I* can be asserted, not only by the *I* in the *I* itself, but also asserted because they are reciprocally limitable, according to the two-folded way of the *theoretical* ("the *I* asserts itself as limited by the *not-I*" aspect upon which is devoted the first part of *The Science of the Right*),[120] and the *practical* ("The *I* asserts the *not-I* as limited by the *I*"). [121] To this second determination—which is the dynamic active transformation of the *not-I* on the historical-empirical level—is devoted the second part of *The Science of the Right*. The *I* is indeed active towards the *not-I*, practically

---

[118] A. Philonenko, *La liberté humaine dans la philosophie de Fichte*, cit., p. 149.
[119] The author's use of *Ichneit* is meant as the "*I*" as a principle, as an absolute subject.
[120] J.G. Fichte, *Fondamento dell'intera dottrina della scienza*, p. 215.
[121] Ibid., p. 213.

transforming it in view of the relation with itself and is, at the same time, passive towards the remaining reality that necessarily asserts the *not-I*, being *ipso facto* determined by it.[122]

In the light of this cursory overview of some of the decisive turning points of *The Science of the Right*, the sense of the second part of Fichte's work should surface more clearly—with its assumption of the actuality of the empirical *Is*—as the theoretical foundation of the lectures on *The Vocation of the Scholar*, by revealing that inseparable nexus—upon which we have already focused our attention many times—between the theoretical structure of the *Wissenschaftslehre* and the sociopolitical structure of the mission of the scholar.[123] The active transformation of the existing *status quo* by the *I*'s praxis so that the *not-I* meets *I*'s principles, represents indeed, from Fichte's point of view, the social mission of man and, at the same time, of the intellectual as man's culturally advanced guide.[124] According to what is clarified in the 1794 first lecture on *The Vocation of the Scholar*, "he [man] exists, that he may become ever morally better himself, and make all around him *physically*, and if he be considered as a member of society, *morally* better also."[125]

The intellectual, from this point of view, is not the bearer of a different vocation compared to the one of man's (opening topic—it is not a coincidence—of the 1794 *Vorlesungen*): Simply, the intellectual has to make the other human beings aware by means of culture of the mission that they all share and make of them only one subject (mankind transcendentally conceived as *Ich*), so that they too, can cooperate in view of a

---

[122] On this matter, the author refers to Manuel Roy, *La doctrine de la science de Fichte: idéalisme spéculatif et réalisme pratique*, (Paris: L'Harmattan, 2010).

[123] See David James, *Fichte's Social and Political Philosophy: Property and Virtue*, (Cambridge: Cambridge University Press, 2011).

[124] See Bernanrd Willms, *Die totale Freiheit. Fichtes politische Philosophie*, (Köln-Opladen: Westdeutscher Verlag, 1967).

[125] J.G. Fichte, *The Vocation of the Scholar*, Lecture I.

common duty that humanity takes up for itself. In this lies the prerogative of the "duty" as a goal that the community of the finite rational beings gives to itself. In the focal point of the never-ending clash between the two counterposed absolute principles, a space is established wherein humanity, as the union between the "empirical *Is*," can always fight off and remove the "empirical *not-Is*" by practically acting in view of the uninterrupted world's transformation according to that duty, which inexhaustibility is guaranteed by the first and the second principle of the *Wissenschaftslehre*.

Free from any alleged thing-in-itself ("the thing *per se* is a mere invention and it is not real," as it will be claimed in the 1797 *First Introduction to Science [Erste Einleitung in die Wissenschaftslehre]*), the dialectic launched in *The Science of the Right* becomes the "skeleton" that holds up the flesh of a philosophical science *(philosophische Wissenschaft)* centered in the unity between subject and object.[126] If the "formal logic" represents that *The Science of the Right's* use of the thought's categories, and stands upon the preventive methodological separation between form and content, Fichte's *Wissenschaftslehre*, for its part, is presented as philosophical science that is at the same time method and content ("Hence, the first principle of *Wissenschaftslehre* must have both content and form")[127] and that supposes an organic (ontological-dialectical) relation between subject—which makes projects, takes action and transforms the totality of its own objectivations—and object that is modified in a programmatic refusal of assuming the world as it is:

---

[126] "Das Ding an sich ist eine blosse Erdichtung, und hat gar keine Realität": J.G. Fichte, *Erste Einleitung in die Wissenschaftslehre*, 1797; ed. and translation by C. Cesa, *Prima introduzione alla Dottrina della scienza*, in Id., *Prima e Seconda Introduzione alla dottrina della scienza*, (Rome-Bari: Laternza, 1999), p. 13.

[127] J.G. Fichte, *Concerning the Conception of the Science of Knowledge Generally*, 1794, Wikisource.

*The I posits against and in front of an object (Gegestand)
wherever it may posit it for the infinity, and in doing so,
posits an activity external to itself and dependent not
upon its activity (of positing) rather on an activity
counterposed to its.[128]*

Hence, the third principle of *Wissenschaftslehre* becomes the
theoretical platform upon which is established the ideal of the
mission of both scholar and—more in general—man, finding
such within its own theoretical basis. The first and the second
principle, for their parts, guarantee the form of this mission
with its configuration of an always reiterated effort because
structurally endless.

By developing under the aspect of time (*sub specie temporis*)
in the concrete dimension of the community activity, the
Wissenschaftslehre's principles—the first of the lectures on the
Mission of the Scholar— teaches that "man is because he is."
He apparently exists as a piece of data (*datum*), like any other
perceivable object. Nevertheless, inasmuch as there is in man
an incurable contrast between sensitivity and reason, by
means of which the former leads him in the world of nature and
mechanism, while the latter elevates and makes him
autonomous and free, the formula "man is because he is" turns
into the formula "man shall be what he is because he is
(reason)."

Not *being*, but *becoming*, and more precisely asymptotically
approaching the conformity with itself, is the proper duty of
man taken into consideration both on the individual level as
well as on the social one. "To be" has to give way to "shall be,"
to the futurizing boost of the always renewable transcending of
the perimeters of the "it-is-so" which, through practical action
leads us towards an unreachable Ithaca, and is nevertheless
ontologically possible and morally necessary: Conformity to
mankind, which is the full unfolding of the ontological

---

[128] J.G. Fichte, *Fondamento dell'intera dottrina della scienza*, p. 501. English
translation by A. Carnesecchi..

possibilities of mankind as *I* as a unitary and undivided subject. According to a splendid passage of the 1794 second lectures on the *Essence of the Scholar* (that will recur almost unvaried in the *Speeches to the German Nation* "whoever thou art—may each of us say—whoever thou art, if thou bear the form of man, thou art a member of this great commonwealth."[129]

From a different perspective, it is the transformative effort rather than the dead objectivity that characterizes the human reality. *Being*, the prosaic monotony of the "it-is-so," the pure factual existence, puts nature and man on the same level of mechanic necessity and spiritual freedom, a factual positivity which sticks to the present time and a transforming praxis which projects itself into the future. Thus, the *I* that we are is a value because it is reason, according to Kant's teaching, but it is a value and reason because it makes itself, creates itself, and projects itself by transcending what it is, in its own cause (*I's causa sui*). It is not indeed "to be" (*esse*), rather it is to become (*fieri*) projected into the dimension of the "not-yet," and it is so because its essence lies not in the "to be," but in the "to do" (*operari*), in the free, creative, and autonomous *Tathandlung* (action) that asserts itself and the social being.

Fichte's apparently only gnoseological controversy against Kant's "thing-in-itself" actually hides a titanic rebellion against the assumption—ideologically characterized—of the social world as a given fact, as a thing-in-itself, given and positive, rather than an object that stands in opposition, namely the result of the social praxis that, as asserted, can always be practically removed and substituted by objectivations more and more in line with the active and thoughtful subjectivity.

As Cesa highlighted, for Fichte the "thing-in-itself" is "a ghost that needs to be removed in order to secure freedom," namely for releasing praxis from any given dead positivity. [130]

---

[129] J.G. Fichte, *The Vocation of the Scholar*, Lecture II.
[130] C. Cesa, *J.G. Fichte e l'idealismo trascendentale*, p. 134.

Fichte addresses the reader in such a way as to demonstrate the independence and freedom gained through the removal of the dogmatism of the "thing-in-itself," and "that reality that you believed you had already glimpsed, a sensible world that exists independently from you, of which you were afraid of becoming slave, disappeared for you."[131] It is in this sense, after all, that for Fichte, the transcendental idealism takes the shape of a philosophy of freedom *par excellence* that consciously opts for the assumption of the *I* as a free principle able to posit itself and objectivity:

> *The essence of critical philosophy consists in this, that the absolute* I *is asserted as absolutely unconditioned and not determinable by anything higher; and if this philosophy draws the consequences from this fundamental principle, then becomes doctrine of knowledge.*[132]

From here, precisely, the "effort" (*Streben*), the strain for creation and for one's own self-planning is aimed at a condition that does not coincide with the actual one, in the form of becoming what one virtually is (on the individual level as well as *a fortiori* on the universal level of mankind). It is superfluous to highlight that this is not the case of an unconditioned creation, because nature exists and is, to a certain extent, given. Rather, it is creation in the dimension of the social being, creation that since it arises, becomes conditioning and emancipates from the nature and, more generally, from the dead positivity of the existing reality, of what actually is.

In a similar perspective, the convergence between the *Wissenschaftslehre*'s genesis and the French Revolution is blatant: as the second sets humanity free from tyranny and chains, thus—according to Fichte's reasoning—*Wissenschafts-*

---

[131] *GA*, I, 6, p. 252. English translation by A. Carnesecchi.
[132] J.G. Fichte, *Werke. Auswahl in sechs Bänden*, cit., I, p. 134. English translation by A. Carnesecchi.

lehre liberates mankind from the fatalism of "the thing-in-itself" and codifies the brave work of a humanity that fights non-stop in order to fully correspond to itself, namely to gain the status of an end in and of itself, in the form of a free, autonomous self-development and, therefore, no longer hetero-directed. Indeed, in radical but certainly not misleading terms, one could uphold that the *Wissenschaftslehre* is going to be an ontologization of the French Revolution, that is a transposition on the ontological level of the historical level of the Revolution as a great overcoming through the transforming praxis of the *I*'s objectivations.[133] The ontologization is namely the titanic gesture of a humanity not meant anymore as a passive theater of tyrannical activity. Rather, it is meant as revolutionary subjectivity that takes action in the theater of the history, so that the several objectivations that it had produced may be removed, transformed, and reconfigured in view of its gradual adaptation to the reason of the acting subjectivity.[134] As Buhr underlined, "Fichte's conception, according to which everything comes from man's free, creative activity (*freie schöpferische Tat*), is a certainty that he acquired especially in relation with his treatise on the French Revolution," besides his discovery of Kant's practical reason.[135]

On the one hand, Fichte glimpses in the events that frantically occur in revolutionary France the evidence of his view of man as the maker (*homo faber*), able to act with absolute freedom and to actively determine the existing reality.

---

[133] On this point, please see the following studies: P.P. Druet, *La politisation de la métaphysique idéaliste. Le cas de Fichte*, in "Revue philosophique de Louvain," 1974, pp. 678-711; F.L. Lendvai, *Die Wissenschaftslehre Fichtes im Zusammenhang mit seiner Geschichts- und Religionsphilosophie*, in "Fichte-Studien," n. 11 (1997), pp. 229-240.

[134] Especially, Tom Rockmore highlighted the importance of the transforming praxis in Fichte's thought, showing the continuity that, in this respect, links Marx to Fichte. See Rockmore – D. Breazeale (ed. by), *Fichte. Historical Contexts, Contemporary Controversies, Humanities*, (Highlands, 1994). See also C. Preve, *Ripensare Marx. Filosofia, idealismo, materialismo*, (Potenza: Ermes, 2007).

[135] M. Buhr, *Revolution und Philosophie. Die französische Revolution und die ursprüngliche Philosophie Fichtes*, p. 106.

On the other hand, Fichte comes to outline the structures of *Wissenschaftslehre* in the form of a transposition on the theoretical-anthropological level of the Revolution. Far from being the product of an abstract utopianism, disconnected from both social and political ground, Fichte's philosophy "represents the theoreticalization of a historical consciousness (*Theoretisierung eines geschichtlichen Bewusstseins*)." [136] As Giuseppe Duso highlighted, "Fichte's relation with the Revolution appears to be very strong, in the two-folded sense that the historical event is seen by the philosopher through the eyes of his rising conception of man, and that his own speculative process is moved and challenged by theoretical interrogatives on the revolution." [137] In a clearer and more effective way, Duso specifies:

In Fichte's conceptual laboratory, wherein the structure of the Doctrine of Knowledge was emerging, Fichte's reflection upon the French Revolution had played a fruitful role both for the centrality given to the concept of freedom and I's independence, and for the acknowledgement, by means of the thematization of the constitution's genesis, of the priority of action over form, acknowledgment that will be speculatively consolidated in the position, within the first principle, not so much of a fact, but of pure action (Tathandlung).[138]

---

[136] Ibid., p. 11.

[137] Giuseppe Duso, *Libertà e Stato in Fichte: la teoria del contratto sociale*, in Id. (ed. by), *Il contratto sociale nella filosofia politica moderna*, (Bologna: Il Mulino, 1987), p. 274. See also M. Giubilato, *Rivoluzione, costituzione e società nel Fichte del '93*, in AA. VV., *Il concetto di rivoluzione nel pensiero politico moderno*, (Bari: De Donato, 1979), pp. 103-138: The author shows the nexus between the Revolution and Fichte's thoughts developing process whose peak is represented by his *Doctrine of Science*. English translation by A. Carnesecchi.

[138] G. Duso, *Libertà e Stato in Fichte: la teoria del contratto sociale*, p. 284. English translation by A. Carnesecchi.

It follows that the *Wissenschaftslehre's not-I* becomes a metaphor, not only of the feudal-lordship society, but also all of the obstacles that hinder *I*'s full unfolding of the human freedom along the mobile line of history: According to what Fichte had programmatically claimed, "our idealism is not dogmatic but practical (*unser Idealismus nicht dogmatisch, sondern praktisch ist*)."[139] We can, therefore, agree with Buhr's opinion, according to which "the French Revolution issues are for Fichte the fundamental problem also in his theoretical philosophy" that is its original codification on the speculative level.[140] Evidence of this is, after all, the fact that in 1795, Fichte's *Contribution* was reprinted such as it was without changes, permeated with the revolutionary pathos which also characterized his *Lectures on the Scholar*.

In Fichte's perspective, at the center of the *Lectures on the Intellectual* and of the 1794-1795 *The Basis of Natural Law* (*Fundamental Principles of the Whole Doctrine of Knowledge*), a value is, therefore, everything that is our creation since it always has traces of rationality, even in forms not always fully transparent or immediately evident. A non-value is, instead all the rest, what is beyond our transforming praxis, including the very same rough fact of our physical existence. It is in the social being's dimension then, that mankind's transformative effort, aimed at a complete transformation in social subjectivity of the social world's non-objective objectivity, can be achieved.

Also, in his lectures on the intellectual, Fichte cannot think of any other rational explanation of "nature"—generically meant as something to counterpose the *I* with—than the one systematically outlined in the *Wissenschaftslehre*. The function

---

[139] J.G. Fichte, *Foundations of Theoretical Knowledge*, edited and translated by Peter Heath and John Lachs, Charles Taylor Editor, (Cambridge: Cambridge University Press, 1982), p. 147. Fichte takes on as a cornerstone of his system that "transforming praxis" of which Marx's thought, especially the eleventh of his *Thesen über Feuerbach*, will show an influence as much evident as unknown.

[140] M. Buhr, *Revolution und Philosophie. Die französische Revolution und die ursprüngliche Philosophie Fichtes*, p. 94. English translation by A. Carnesecchi.

of *not-I* is to stimulate our moral activity to rise and persist, and exists because of the *I*, and more precisely because of the free unfolding of man's mission meant as a self-enhancing activity in the titanic fight against the objectivity that is always to be, all over again, removed. Without obstacle, there would be no effort, and without effort, moral action would not be possible. The intellectual's duty as outlined in the lectures lies indeed in guiding mankind on the tortuous journey that leads him to fully coincide with himself, making it possible that man becomes man, namely coinciding in the very act (*in actu*) with his own potential general nature.

"Man, be man!" is the apparently tautological form of the imperative—to actually become what one can potentially be— that Fichte gives each of us. The imperative is that the intellectual, with his own knowledge applied on the practical-transformative ground, allows one to apply on society the only space in which the process of gradual conformation to mankind is possible. Man, as a matter of fact, does not live in hieratic loneliness; neither can he (against Kant's transcendental solipsism) become accomplished in isolation because by his own nature, man is a social being, a being who naturally lives with others (topic to which is devoted the third lecture and upon which Fichte will insist a few years later in his *Basis of Natural Law*). The *I* is always a social, collective *I*, metaphor of the unity of the genre transcendentally meant as a singular-collective subject.[141]

From a different perspective, if Kant's ethics remain confined at the stage of the autonomous individual—a practical version of the transcendental apperception—Fichte's ethics is instead heteronomous, because it is social morality that is ethical, and the social ethics of a man who takes action through society, who only within society can morally become accomplished by transforming himself and the ethical world in which it is projected. Only in this light, after all, is it possible

---

[141] See R. Lauth, *Le problème de l'interpersonnalité chez Fichte*, in "Archives de Philosophie," July–December 1962, pp. 325-344.

to understand the 1798 passages from *Lectures on the Theory of Ethics*, in which Fichte critically examines the abstract formalism of Kant's ethics by opposing it to social ethics, that it has a concrete meaning. In what Pareyson has labeled as a "very decisive claim of sociality and action," [142] Fichte's constant reference remains the *Congregation of I's (Gemeinde von Ichen)*: In his opinion, "man becomes man only among men," [143] as "the individual exists just as a part, by virtue and in view of a wholeness" coinciding with the ethical community. [144] Pareyson significantly wrote in relation to Fichte's social perspective:

> *The concept of finite spirit is the one of a totality that is in reciprocal relation with itself, namely it is divided in elements that mutually integrate. The individual is such only within society, and society is necessary totality. Individuality arises as a concept essentially linked with the one of totality.* [145]

As has been noticed by the critique, if it is true that since the 1794 lectures on the intellectual, the social nature of the rational being (that, by the way, emerged in a not at all marginal way even in the *Revolutionary Writings*) is largely codified, then "We need to wait for the *Foundation of Natural Right* to find a detailed analysis of this topic. This will not be abandoned, as the contemporary developments that appear in the *Foundations of Transcendental Philosophy New Method*

---

[142] L. Pareyson, *Fichte: il sistema della libertà*, p. 260. English translation by A. Carnesecchi.
[143] J.G. Fichte, *Werke. Auswahl in sechs Bänden*, cit., II, pp. 34. English translation by A. Carnesecchi.
[144] Id., *Nachgelassene Schriften* (= NS), ed. by H. Jacob, II, Schriften aus den Jahren 1790-1800, (Berlin, 1937), p. 515. English translation by A. Carnesecchi.
[145] L. Pareyson, *Fichte: il sistema della libertà*, p. 382. English translation by A. Carnesecchi.

(*Wissenschaftslehre nova method*) show."[146] The social thought —this is the decisive point—will never leave Fichte's philosophy; on the contrary, it will be Fichte's persistent and central point of his thought to such an extent that it would not indeed be misleading to think of Fichte, according to Aldo Masullo's valuable suggestion, as a community thinker.[147]

According to what has been clarified in the third lecture on the *Essence of the Scholar*, man is destined to live in society in order to unfold his own duty of self-enhancement and improvement of society as a whole. As underlined by these basic principles (*grundzüge*), man is called to do so by spreading his own idea and therefore, making everyone do the same so that through freedom, all relations according to reason can be socially established ("Reason always proceeds with freedom"). [148] For Fichte, the ethics of an inward-looking individual would simply be immoral. From this assumption can be coherently drawn the consequence, according to which the scholar meant as *scholar*, must leave space for the scholar meant as *intellectual*.[149]

It is a decisive point upon which *The Lectures* emphatically insist. The moral law imposes that the social instinct does not contradict itself, but this contradiction would naturally occur if we considered *the others* as *others from ourselves*—this is the point—as indifferent to morality—or even worse, according to what Kant had highlighted already—if we only considered them as means for our actions. Thus, in the time of abstract

---

[146] C. De Pascale, *Etica e diritto: la filosofia pratica di Fichte e le sue ascendenze kantiane*, p. 200. English translation by A. Carnesecchi.

[147] See A. Masullo, *Fichte: l'intersoggettività e l'originario*, (Naples: Guida, 1986): in particular Masullo is convinced that "it is not possible to critically talk about the human origin of the world, if it is not understood the social origin of humanity. Fichte is the philosopher of freedom but, for him, the latter is essentially inter-subjective" (ibid., p. 7). Fichte, argues Masullo, since the first works explicitly aim at "overcoming the individualism that is abstractly plural in a human social environment" (ibid., p. 40).

[148] J.G. Fichte, *The Scholar's Vocation*, Lecture II.

[149] See P.L. Oesterreich, *Die Einheit der Lehre ist der Gelehrte selbst. Zur personalen Idee der Philosophie bei Johann Gottlieb Fichte*, in "Fichte-Studien," n. 16 (1999), pp. 1-18.

reflection, this would mean servilely conforming to the widespread egoism of the "accomplished sinfulness" (*vollendete Sündhaftigkeit*) according to Fichte's splendid formula in his *Characteristics of the Present Age.* [150] In other words, by following Fichte's reasoning, evidence of our own freedom must be considered in the fact that we glimpse around us free beings in the certainty—equally expressed by both Hegel and Marx—that one can be really free only if everybody is free, namely only if freedom becomes a universal principle that actually permeates the structures of the social world. "He only is *free,*" writes Fichte, "who would make all around him free likewise."[151] This is another way to say that freedom can only exist universally, and therefore, as liberation from the residual forms of subjection and as praxis that imposes universal freedom posited by the reason itself and its unexhausted attempt to titanically conform the *not-I* to itself.

The moral law, by aiming at the total formal harmony with ourselves, prioritizes the need of overcoming and conciliating the individual differences that spring from the empirical differences of the diverse human beings and not from the rational principle (the pure *I*) that lies in all of us. The overcoming and reconciliation of the differences occurs on the social level in an ideal of unity and rational harmony of society meant as free and equal development of all of its members, by means of the self-acknowledgement of humanity as a unitary subject. This is a pure ideal that will be not achievable once and for all because, if so, this ideal would reduce to dead positivity, to something "practico-inert," as Sartre would say in his *Critique of Dialectical Reason* (*Critique de la raison dialectique*), namely an objectivity that needs the constant

---

[150] J.G. Fichte, *Characteristics of the Present Age*, 1806, Wikisource. The third age of the *Grundzüge*—"the accomplished sinfulness"—is traceable, even though drafted in a different manner, in the 1813 *Doctrine of the State*, since Fichte speaks about the age of luxury and egoism that is characterized by having lost the holy as well as the social connection typical of a community.
[151] J.G. Fichte, *The Vocation of the Scholar*, Lecture II.

renovation of our social effort under the guidance of the intellectual.

The *not-I* as *nature* produces physical inequality, and as *social objectivations* cause social inequality, it follows that *I* must oppose *not-I* by taking on equality as the end of the moral action guided and always guarded by the intellectual, according to what has been unequivocally specified in the third lecture. In this sense, the equality that rationalistic naturalism posits as a starting point, is taken on by Fichte as the arrival point of a historical process characterized by efforts, fights, and practical determination, by means of which humanity overcomes obstacles that it places between itself and its complete and free self-acknowledgment as a unitary mankind. Thus, in this way, history becomes the theater of a process of alienation and reconciliation, in which mankind places itself in the objectivity and non-objectivity of the social dimension, through the never-ending effort of overcoming the obstacles, acquiring a clearer self-consciousness, closer and closer (even if never coincidental with) the complete harmony between subjectivity and objectivity.

It is, after all, within this horizon of meaning that the stinging controversy against Rousseau finds its place at the core of the fifth lecture on *The Scholar*. For Fichte, at the origin of mankind there is no equality—later shattered by the egoism that followed according to Rousseau's belief; on the contrary, originally there is inequality, in which respect the dynamic of man's becoming man (that coincides with the historical adventures of mankind) is nothing but a slow and never-ending process of departure from its original condition. It is not in the past (Rousseau), but in a constantly deferred future (Fichte) that the transforming praxis is always active, in which lies the perfection of mankind.

From here, the supremacy of Fichte's practical reason descends: A supremacy that surely follows Kant's lesson, but which already marks an irremediable departure from it, if we consider that Fichte's practicality is already socially and practically characterized, and no more confined within the moral action domain of the singular individual, who in his loneliness, autonomously follows duty for duty's sake.[152] As Roger Garaudy highlighted, "Fichte goes beyond Kant for a further reason: The practical reason has not only a moral but also a social character. Man is destined to live in society" in order to unfold through society the practical aspect in which its essence is condensed.[153]

Philosophy, then—and this is the core of Fichte's message—is not to be abstractly theorized, but it needs to be lived, practised, and acted. The intellectual must, therefore, be the dogged defender of the spirituality against the vulgar, materialist hedonism of the cosmos of goods fetishistically absolutized. He must tirelessly spread—against the reconciled morality of the lazy and inert spirits—the fever of the action of those who, perennially dissonant with the world order, do not passively accept something existing *per se*, as objectivity irremediably objective. With Fichte's words:

> *In the domain of what I call philosophy there cannot be anything static, immobile, and dead. In philosophy everything is action, movement, and life (ist alles That, Bewegung und Leben); philosophy does not find anything but makes everything to rise under its own eyes, and this at the extent that I entirely refuse to call philosophy that business with dead concepts.[154]*

---

[152] See D. Breazeale, *Der fragwürdige "Primat der praktischen Vernunft"* in *Fichte's Grundlage der gesamten Wissenschaftslehre*, in *"Fichte-Studien,"* n. 10 (1997), pp. 253-271.
[153] Roger Garaudy, *Clefs pour Marx*, 1972; Italian translation and edited by di M. Feldbauer, *Karl Marx*, (Milan: Sonzogno, 1974), p. 48. English translation by A. Carnesecchi.
[154] J.G. Fichte, *Aus einem Privatschreiben*, January, 1800, in *GA*, I, 6, pp. 372-374; Italian translation by G. Moretto, *Da una lettera privata del gennaio 1800*, in Id., *La dottrina della religione*, (Naples: Guida, 1989,) p. 227. English translation by A. Carnesecchi.

♦

Whoever believes in spirituality and in the freedom of this spirituality; and who wills the eternal development of this spirituality by freedom, wherever he may have been born and whatever language he speaks, is of our blood; he is one of us, and will come over to our side.

J.G. Fichte, *Addresses to the German Nation*

♦

However, the *I* (Ego) should be absolute and totally posited by itself. If it (Ego) is posited by the *not-I*, it does not posit itself and will be in contradiction with the highest and absolutely first principle. In order to avoid this contradiction, we need to assume that the *not-I*, which has to posit the intelligence, may be posited by the *I*, which in this role would not be the subject that represents, but it would have an absolute causality.

J.G. Fichte, *On the Concept of the Science of Knowledge*

♦

4.

The Content of the Lectures on the Scholar

♦

After this first formative review, and after having outlined the inescapable links with *Wissenschaftslehre*, we can finally try to analytically focus on the contents of each of the 1794 lectures.

First Lecture:

The Vocation of Man as Such

◆

In cohesion with the primary practical vocation of reason codified on the theoretical level, in the preface Fichte clarifies that the aim of his lectures is not abstract, contemplative theory, but active transformation of reality in view of its harmonization with reason, namely the *not-I* transformed in view of its adjustment to the *I*, and not *vice versa*, according to the dogmatism at the heart of the harsh invective of the *First Introduction to Science* which followed in 1797. It is a goal that is all the more difficult if one considers that the time period which in great measure opens up with 1789 tends to be gravitationally reabsorbed into the inertia and resigned acceptance of "this is it." Even though dogmatic fatalists in each time period are undoubtedly the majority, Fichte points out that never before in actual circumstance has this majority been so overwhelming in extent that envisioning the practicality of change became even more remote.

Against the ancient and new dogmatists, the intellectual at the center of Fichte's lectures is heartily called upon to assert the principle of dissonance with the existing reality, which is the engine of the transforming praxis. "The Actual must be judged by the Ideal, and modified in accordance with it by those who feel themselves capable of such a task," programmatically claims the philosopher in what could be rightly considered one of the main "design signatures" of his thought, beside the place where the unavoidable nexus between his lectures and the third principle of the 1794-1795 *The Science of the Right* shines through the most.[155] It is in here that the icastic secret of these pages lies, which does not make peace with the world: The project is aimed at the perfection of mankind.[156]

Hence, the *Lectures'* preface outlines a horizon of meaning in which the lectures are structured, drafting in broad terms the premises of an ontology of praxis—founded on the principles of *Wissenschaftslehre*, perennially unreconciled with the existing reality—which aims at a kind of rationality that is still missing. In order to unfold itself, the ontology of praxis needs also the action of a society guided by intellectuals. Fichte knows well that to the ideal, in the name of which it is necessary to act in order to enhance its level to the level of reality, the time that lends itself to the logic of an intrinsic cohesion to the existing reality (in the forms of the Empiricism and Utilitarianism which are essentially correlated with each other) is totally indifferent. Besides those who disregard the ideas of "rejuvenation of the world," there are also those, as the author outlines, "who hold such speculations at best useless, because they cannot be carried out into practice, and because they find nothing in the actual world, as it is now constituted, at all corresponding thereto." [157] In reading such a fiery premise, comes to mind a *Contribution*'s passage that, with a similar tone, had insisted upon the general refusal (especially by the ruling power) to accept this praxis to be guided by the philosophical principles:

---

[155] J.G. Fichte, *The Vocation of the Scholar*, Preface.
[156] Ibid.
[157] Ibid.

However, you keep on saying that our philosophical principles cannot be adapted to life; that our theories are certainly unconfutable, but cannot be applied. Well, that means that this is your judgment because you always evaluate under the condition "if everything must remain as it is now." Otherwise, your claim would be too self-confident. But who did say that everything must remain so? However, you want that everything graciously remains like in the past. From here your resistance, from here your clamor on the impossibility to apply our principles. Now, be at least sincere, and do not say anymore: "we cannot put in practice your principles," but say out loud what you think: "we do not want to put them in practice."[158]

On the basis of this premise (that is nothing but a recapitulation written in the form of an introduction to *Lectures'* publication), the first lecture starts off with plenty of interconnected questions which in fact coincide with the enunciation of the topics that will be unfolded in the course of the *Lectures*: "What is the vocation of the scholar?" and "what is his relation to Humanity as a whole, as well as to particular classes of men?"[159] The figure, and thus the function of the intellectual can be derived only by contrast, that is in terms of genus and the specific difference of an associate (*per genus proximum et differentiam specificam*) compared to he who is not an intellectual.[160] Hence, from this determination, it clearly emerges that the scholar cannot but be defined by his

---

[158] SW, VI, p. 71, English translation by A. Carnesecchi.
[159] Fichte, *The Vocation of the Scholar*, I lecture.
[160] This Latin formula: *"definitio fit per genus proximum et differentiam specificam"* recaps the Scholasticism's criteria of definition. Starting by citing from the genre (both scholar and intellectual belong to mankind), to then specify the differences between the two. The difference between man and intellectual is the function of the latter of transforming the society in which he lives.

unbreakable nexus with society, of which he is both an integral part and an active transformer of it by means of culture.

His role, however, does not uniquely come from his link with culture. On the contrary, to make him an intellectual is actually the use he makes of culture in relation to society. In Fichte's words: "the vocation of the scholar [here meant as intellectual] as such is only conceivable in society," upon which he actively differentiates the way of his culture, given that he is the holder, by placing it in the service of society's emancipation. [161] Emancipation can be achieved exclusively through the active circulation of the knowledge and of the education and training (*Bildung*), so that each member of society may be able to freely give his contribution, through a conscious involvement, to the duty of the unlimited perfecting of society.

The question of the distinction between intellectual and non-intellectual, however, raises a further question that is actually upstream, from which the answer depends also upon the question regarding the nature of the scholar. What is the vocation of man in society? Also, after all, such a question refers to another equally important interrogative: What is the vocation of man as such? Only by answering these questions in their reciprocal references does it become possible to clarify who is an intellectual and what his specific role is within society, contrasted with the vocation of man as such, and taking this into consideration because of his action in society. It is for this reason that the first lecture is devoted to the vocation of man as a privileged way through which to decipher the scholar's mission, as will be outlined in the following lecture. In the light of these considerations, the nexus between the 1794 Lecture on the intellectual and the following *The Vocation of Man* (1800) appears to be, thereon, blatant.

In large part, the first lecture diffusely unfolds in a better articulated way the themes that were already at the heart of

---

[161] J.G. Fichte, *The Vocation of the Scholar*, Lecture I.

the *Revolutionary Writings*, in particular the idea that man's vocation corresponds to the transforming praxis, with the sociomoral enhancement that proceeds infinitely ([*ins Unendliche*], and thereon has also the right to oppose with violence whatever may hinder this unlimited and limitless movement).

The two questions previously stated regarding man (what is the vocation of man as such, and as part of society) do, in fact, coincide. The mission of man himself would not unfold if it were not for his concrete action in the social dimension. The intellectual, for his part, is called to take on the difficult role of a guide of humanity, spurring it to act in view of this goal, because the intellectual is no one but he who is able to decipher the structure of reality, the arduous and difficult modelling of the *not-I* by the *I* through social praxis. His knowledge is, for this very reason, immediately a practical transformation.

The vocation of man and the vocation of the intellectual coincide (as Fichte himself admits in the first lecture: "What is the vocation of the scholar [intellectual]—or what is the same thing, as will appear in due time, the vocation of the highest truest man?").[162] However, if you prefer, the specificity of *The Vocation of the Scholar* lies in the fact that he must make man aware of his mission through culture. Considering man in himself—the topic of the lecture—means not to consider the *pure I* (*Absolute I*) of the first principle of the *Wissenschaftslehre*, but the *empirical I*, the particular individual and, at the same time, the community as an organic totality of individuals, namely the third principle of science. There is a comparison between man and reason (when it is free from any external influence): They both are their own ends.

Still, inasmuch as man is an unstable mix of sensibility and reason, his aim thereby (*eo ipso*), coincides not with *be*, but with *ought-to-be* that is imposed by his rational nature. Not the actuality, but the repeated overcoming of such, guards the

---

[162] J.G. Fichte, *The Vocation of the Scholar*, Lecture I.

secret of the "mission-vocation" (*Beruf*) of man. The coincidence with himself is not something given, but needs to be achieved through transformative effort (of himself and of the existing reality); in other terms, the *empirical I* must aim at the condition of the *pure I*, pure activity and harmonious unity, by overcoming the multiple contradictions and therefore aligning what is not rational, the *not-I*, to oneself ("so I denominate everything which is conceived of as existing external to the Ego [*I*], distinguished from, and opposed to it").[163] Because the will is free while the sensibility depends on objects, one needs to make an impact on objects and dominate the sensibility that still we are, and we cannot help not to be. This is, after all, the most authentic duty of culture. Fichte explains that culture "is the last and highest means to the attainment of the great end of man, when he is considered as of a composite nature, rational and sensuous."[164]

It is in here that, once again lying on the level of the third principle of *Wissenschaftslehre*, the mission of the *I* is reproposed: The supreme good towards which we aim as human beings coincides with the complete harmony with ourselves, namely—this is the point—with the condition of the *pure I* (pure unity of man's goal which is, in itself, harmonious, indivisible, and acting as a unique subject). Nevertheless, it is a structurally unachievable aim towards which we still have to tend through always renewed efforts. The mission of man is identified then with a never-ending self-perfecting work that, in order to unfold, implies the active overcoming of the concrete crystallizations in which action sets down (the non-objective objectivity of the social world).

In order to understand this crucial point, it is necessary to refer again to the *Wissenschaftslehre* and resolutely oppose the dogmatism that makes man depend on the external world, the *I* on the *not-I*: "It is not indeed true that the pure Ego [*I*] is a

---

163 Ibid.
164 Ibid.

product of the Non-Ego [*not-I*]," explains Fichte.[165] Certainly, man—every man—is also the *not-I*, in so far as he is subjected to empirical determinations of both natural and social kinds (firstly, because he has a body). Well, in the light of the aporetic coexistence of nature and reason within a human being, man exists, but he must become himself in achieving the morally necessary conformity to the ontological possible genre. This is another way to say that reason must triumph upon *not-I*, by imposing its own seal. Once again, man is an end in himself and does not exist in view of something external, but in view of his correspondence with himself to freely unfold his ontological potentialities, and also to achieve that condition of full acknowledgement of mankind as the only transcendental subject taking action in the world as well as in history: "His being is its own ultimate object."[166] Man is not yet what must (morally) be and can (ontologically) be.

Man's ontological status is acknowledged, therefore, to be structurally ambiguous. He is one sensible being among many, a purely existing determination; nevertheless, his brute being is not the whole of his essence. From a different perspective, as empirical fact *he is*, but as moral spirituality, *he must be*; because of the fact that he is, he must perfect himself in view of his full correspondence with his own reason: "The principle propounded above—man is because he is—is changed into the following—*Whatever Man is, that he should be, solely because he is.*"[167] He must, therefore, be an end in himself by determining himself without being determined by anything else. He must be what he is because he wants to be it freely. In Fichte's own words, "given that man is endowed with reason, he is for himself his own purpose, namely does not exist because of the fact that he must exist as something else, but rather, *vice versa*, he purely exists because he must exist."[168] It

---

[165] Ibid.
[166] Ibid.
[167] Ibid.
[168] Ibid. English translation by A. Carnesecchi.

is from here then, that the praxis' determination starts off directly by referring to the *Wissenschaftslehre*'s theoretical acquisition:

> *Hence it is not the vocation of man to attain this end. But he may and should constantly approach nearer to it: and thus, the unceasing approximation to this end is his true vocation as man (ist die Annäherung ins unendliche zu diesem Ziele seine wahre Bestimmung als Mensch).*[169]

Man exists in order to improve himself more and more (*"perfection* is the highest unattainable *end* of man, whilst *eternal* perfecting is his *vocation"*), to make an effort to perfect himself and all that is around him, finding in society his natural location (*locus naturalis*).[170] Man is, in fact, by nature a social being; he cannot exist by himself nor can he autonomously practice his morality (with all due respect for Kant and for his dismissal of any "heteronomous" instance). The first lecture ends indeed with a breakthrough to the community, with a remarkable apocalyptic tone that emphatically insists upon Fichte's vocation as a teacher and his students as his cooperators in the cultural project of rejuvenation of the world that goes along jointly with the humanity's enhancement.

---

[169] Fichte, *The Vocation of the Scholar*, I lecture.
[170] Ibid.

Second Lecture:

The Vocation of Man in Society

◆

This lecture recalls the themes that have been sketched out in the previous one, stressing the main practical point of Fichte's perspective. The speculation has undoubtedly solved all the problems it could, thanks to "critical philosophers." Only praxis can permit acquiring new theoretical achievements. In Fichte's words, "all questions which still remained unanswered must be answered upon practical principles," making the external world thereon correspond with the I.[171] Using Fichte's words, "every idea that exists in the Ego [I] must have a representative, an antitype in the Non-Ego [not-I]," according to the practical instances of the *Wissenschaftlehre*.[172]

Overall, the second lecture is based on the dynamic connection between two ideas: (a) Man is not an isolated being, but a social subject who lives with his counterparts (with the obvious consequence that only with his counterparts can he fully unfold his own ontological potentialities). (b) The ground of social relations is society: the only place where morality can be expressed (against Kant's transcendental solipsism). From

---

[171] Fichte, *The Vocation of the Scholar*, II Lecture.
[172] Ibid.

a different perspective, rational beings' reciprocal relation coincides with society—that is the acting stage of men, and therefore, their sole possibility of being authentically moral. To characterize, society is first of all freedom, according to the fruitful reference that a single man is free only if society overall is also free and in a symmetrical way, society is free only if its members are completely free.

The lecture starts off with what usually represents the fundamental theme of the *Wissenschaftslehre* since its exposition in *Concerning the Conception of the Doctrine of Knowledge Generally*, (*Uber den Begriff der Wissenschaftlehre*, 1794), which is the attempt to make *scientific* and systematic philosophy's endeavour (*systematically scientific*) by liberating philosophy from its traditional connotation of tension towards a knowledge, longed for because not possessed, without losing its autonomous truthful character. Philosophical knowledge is, in fact, called to solve absolutely and unquestionably—the systematic truth of a sequence of theoretical and practical problems. By overcoming them, they can then "assume the character of knowledge and science," and do so only by keeping a distance from the antithetical of—and therefore, in essential correlation with—*relativist scepticism* and *fatalist dogmatism*.[173]

For Fichte, the main problem which philosophy is called upon to solve in order to reach the level of Science (*Wissenschaft*), the overcoming of which is necessary to even lay the foundation of the "natural law rationally founded" that Fichte will fully codify two years later in his *Basis of Natural Law*), sounds like this:[174] How does man acknowledge that there are external beings other than himself and similar to him (equally moral) if such beings are not immediately given in the pure self-consciousness, but they are given in the deceitful empirical sphere? Only in this way, after all, does it become

---

[173] Ibid.

[174] See Paul Dubouchet, *Philosophie et doctrine du droit chez Kant, Fichte et Hegel,* (Paris: L'Harmattan, 2005).

possible to found the vocation of man in society as an active praxis of transformation of oneself and the others.

Society—insists Fichte—is "the relation of reasonable beings to each other,"[175] namely the nexus that they organically form among themselves according to (the principle of) freedom.[176] Now, the concept itself of society is not possible if it is not founded upon the premise of the existence of others (and therefore of the "acknowledgement" (*Anerkennung*) of rational beings external to us who are, nevertheless, as rational and moral as ourselves. The experience does continuously *show* us that other beings external to us do exist, but it will never be able to *demonstrate* that, to this representation, corresponds something real. That is to say, if in actuality rational beings exist independently from our representation, they are namely beings who may exist and morally and rationally act, regardless of whether we represent them to us as such.

The problem was recently raised by Jacobi who had solved it by relying on faith: "It is by faith that we know that we have a body and that outside ourselves, other bodies and other thinking beings exist. Truthful revelation! Wonderful revelation!"[177] Fichte makes use of Jacobi's formula and at the same time, aims at rationally demonstrating the belief regarding the existence of other complete rational beings. In particular, in order to *demonstrate* what is vaguely attested to by *representation*, Fichte uses a *two-folded argumentative strategy* along conceptual turning points that refer to each other, one of which is the coherent development of the other: (a) If it is true that reason must correspond to reality (in the sense of, as has been said several times, the free transformation of the object according to the principles of the subject), it is also true that in us is firmly rooted the *concept of*

[175] J.G. Fichte, *The Vocation of the Scholar*, Lecture II.
[176] On this aspect, see Axel Honneth, *La necessità trascendentale dell'intersoggettività. Sul secondo teorema del saggio sul diritto naturale di Fichte*, in "Rivista di Filosofia," n. 89 (1998), pp. 213-238.
[177] F.H. Jacobi, *Werke*, ed. by C.J.F. von Roth – F. Köppen, IV, (Leipzig, 1812) ss., p. 210-211. English translation by A. Carnesecchi.

action according to reason, through which we evaluate the actions that the experience has shown us. It is consequently necessary, explains Fichte, that rational beings exist external to us and are bearers themselves of that moral action that we continuously experience around us, of which we are not the creators. (b) If my free action modifies the phenomenon to such an extent that it cannot be expressed as starting from that law to which it previously conformed, but only starting from the one that I freely affected by acting upon, thereon when this process does occur in other situations not directly determined by me, I will equally have to admit, by extension, that there is another rational being who freely imprints his law on the phenomenon exactly as it happened with my own transformative action.

Along this way is rationally founded the existence of other rational beings, avoiding the solipsism and with it, lay the foundations for a "community pervaded by design; and it is this which I call Society."[178] The same tendency to "find" outside ourselves rational beings—a tendency that, strictly speaking, is the reason for the argumentative strategy that we have just traced—corresponds for Fichte to the "social impulse" that is coessential to the fact of being born man, namely the *Vocation of Man in Society*, according to the title of this second lecture. Coherently with this foundation of the sociality of man and his natural vocation to socially living,[179] Fichte devotes a wide parentheses to the nature of man Aristotlically conceived as a political animal (*zoon politikon*);[180] as a sociable, political, and social animal (according to the three inseparable conceptual determinations which are part of the formula in Aristotle's *Politics*), man is called to live in the community, and he is

---

[178] Fichte, *The Vocation of the Scholar*, Lecture II.

[179] See Virginia López-Domínguez, *Individuo y Comunidad: reflexiones sobre el eterno círculo fichteano*, in "Daimon. Revista de Filosofia," n. 11 (1994), pp. 139-154.

[180] "Man is by nature a political animal, and a man that is by nature and not merely by fortune citiless is either low in the scale of humanity or above it": Aristotle, Politica, I A, 2, 1253 a 3.

unable to isolate himself unless through an unnatural separation from the social network of the origin.

The social impulse (der gesellschaftliche Trieb) thus belongs to the fundamental impulses of man. It is man's vocation to live in Society (ist bestimmt, in der Gesellschaft zu leben)—he must live in Society—he is no complete man, but contradicts his own being, if he lives in a state of isolation.[181]

Against the modern "Robesonian" ideology—or the original individual, as Marx will later qualify it (ideology that runs, differently unfolded, from Kant's *ego cogitans* to his *Ich denke)*—Fichte insists on the social matter as a given basis to humanity, according to the theme that runs through Fichte's entire opus, and which perhaps finds its most effective expression in Fichte's *Foundations of Natural Right (Grundlage des Naturrechts)*: "Man attains rights only in a community with others, as indeed he only becomes man [...] through intercourse with others. Man, indeed, cannot be thought as one individual."[182] against the delusive abstractions of those who—following Locke and the *homo oeconomicus'* ideology—imagine as original the isolated single individual who works for himself and perceives reality as a moment altogether secondary and derived from it.[183] Kant himself, after all, meant the social sphere as a completely secondary

[181] J.G. Fichte, *The Vocation of the Scholar*, Lecture II.
[182] J.G. Fichte, *Foundations of Natural Right*, Book Third, *Application of the Conception of Rights*, 1796, Wikisource.
[183] On this topic, this author refers to the following studies: M.H. Kramer, *John Locke and the Origins of Private Property: Philosophical Explorations of Individualism, Community, and Equality*, (Cambridge: Cambridge University Press, 1997); J. Hahn, *Der Begriff des Property bei John Locke. Zu den Grundlagen seiner politischen Philosophie*, (Frankfurt a.M.: Lang, 1984); J.T. Peters, *Der Arbeitsbegriff bei John Locke*, (Münster: LIT, 1997); W. Euchner, *Naturrecht und Politik bei John Locke*, 1969; tr. it. *La filosofia politica di Locke*, (Rome-Bari: Laterza, 1976).

consequence compared to the single *I* as morally autonomous.[184]

Directly after having explained the necessity of living within society as a condition in order to unfold one's own social essence through the "free reciprocal activity" (*Wechselwirkung durch Freiheit*),[185] Fichte clarifies that man is certainly "a social and community-oriented animal," but not a "State animal." To live in society is an aim, while to live in the State is a *means*, so that men not yet endowed with a solid morality may be able to peacefully reach the aim abovementioned.[186] It is in accordance with the theoretical lines of the *Wissenschaftslehre* that Fichte outlines this program of overcoming the form of the State that, by the way, will be integrally taken up and metabolized by Marx himself: Because the history of humanity must be considered as more and more an unfolding of ethics, it follows that humanity, finally moralized, will no longer need to resort to the use of a "coercive instrument" to impose ethics from the outside, by respecting laws that are not felt by the subject himself as cogent. Thus, the aim of every State is to make itself superfluous. Masullo wrote:

> *The ultimate aim of man, his supreme ideal, is the passage from social coexistence to free community. Never had it been underlined before with such a speculative strength and passion the character deeply communitarian, and thereon, ethical, of the human condition: the original inter-subjectivity of man is transfigured into the supreme essence of duty.*[187]

---

[184] It is not that in Kant the theme of the community is naturally missing (see, for instance, in this regard, Pirni, *Kant filosofo della comunità*, Pisa: ETS, 2006): It is, anyway, secondary and not the origin of it, since in Kant's perspective, the origin is the individual and not the community.

[185] J.G. Fichte, *The Vocation of the Scholar*, Lecture, II.

[186] Ibid. See also Luca Fonnesu, *L'ideale dell'estinzione dello Stato in Fichte*, in "*Rivista di Storia della Filosofia*," n. 2 (1996), pp. 257-270.

[187] A. Masullo, *Fichte: l'intersoggettività e l'originario*, p. 140. English translation by A. Carnesecchi.

The theme of the existence of the State ripened in Fichte also because of his attendance at Masonic entourages (Fichte had ties with Masonry since 1793). In particular, it was Lessing in his work, *Conversations for Freemans* (*Gespräche für Freimaurer* 1778-1780), who put at the heart of his reflection the extinction of the State as a condition for humanity's moralization. However, since humanity has not reached full autonomy, the State plays a fundamental role as—according to what Fichte will coherently assert in the pages of *The Closed Commercial State* (*Der geschlossene Handelsstaat*) the last bastion of the hegemony of the political level on the economic one, and therefore of resistance against the commercial entropy and its "evil cosmopolitism," planetary universalization of the egotisms.[188]

With all due respect to the most consolidated interpretations, there is no contradiction within Fichte's system in the passage from the ideal of the State, at the heart of the *Lectures* on the scholar, to the codification of the *Closed Commercial State*. Anyway, there is no rupture or any change of paradigm in the transition to *Speeches to the German Nation* nationalism, inasmuch as in them, the universalism of emancipation keeps on being the aim of thought and action, an aim that is made possible through the concrete action of a population. Humanity in complete autonomy remains an ideal without any State coercion, but a commercially closed and organistically structured State is fundamental to a specific conjuncture for the aim to be realized in a time of completed sinfulness. In such a time, individuals are eradicated from the community and made absolute in an alienated form, which is the form of the *abstractly omnipotent* single person and *concretely impotent* individual, because of being submitted to the overwhelming mechanism of the planetary commercial

---

[188] On these topics that in here can be only mentioned, see Andreas Verzar, *Das autonome Subjekt und der Vernunftstaat: eine [...] Untersuchung zu Fichtes "Geschlossenem Handelstaat,"* (Bonn: Bouvier, 1979).

anarchy.[189] With the splendid words of Spinoza's *Ethics*, "Man who is guided by reason is more free in a State where he lives under a general system of laws than he is living in solitude, where he obeys only himself (*homo qui ratione ducitur, magis in civitate, ubi ex communi decreto vivit, quam in solitudine, ubi sibi soli obtemperat, liber est*)."[190]

The goal of mankind's process of emancipation coincides, thereon, with cosmopolitism—namely a human international community, unitary, organic—without State and morally united.[191] According to what will be asserted in *Characteristics of the Present Age* in a sort of cosmopolitism of emancipation guaranteed by praxis, "the aim of humanity's life on earth is that it may freely establish all its relations according to reason" (*der Zweck des Erdenlebens der Menschheitist der, dass sie in demselben alle ihre Verhaltnisse mit Freiheitnach der Vernunft einrichte*).[192] Against the time of the sinful egoism, Fichte will explain, "life in compliance with reason depends upon the fact that the individual puts his life on the line for the idea,"[193] namely of that free development of mankind (the becoming-man-of man) that guarantees the "compliance with mankind" (*Gattungsmässigkeit*).[194] With Fichte's words: "Humanity's destination is the uninterrupted progress of culture and the uninterrupted homogeneous unfolding of every disposition and need of humanity as such."[195]

The cosmopolitan inflection of Fichte's discourse is once again reflected in the *Wissenschaftslehre*'s principles. A

[189] See Allen W. Wood, *Kant and Fichte on Right, Welfare, and Economic Redistribution*, in "Internationales Jahrbuch des Deutschen Idealismus," n. 2 (2004), pp. 77-101.
[190] Baruch Spinoza, *Ethics Demonstrated in Geometrical Order*, Jonathan Bennett, p. 115.
[191] See G. Duso, *La philosophie politique de Fichte. De la forme juridique à la pensée de la pratique*, in "Les études philosophiques," n. 1 (2001), pp. 49-66.
[192] J.G. Fichte, *Characteristics of the Present Age*.
[193] Ibid. English translation by A. Carnesecchi.
[194] On the concept of "genre" in Fichte, see A. Cantoni, *La filosofia e la teoria della storia in Fichte*, in "Rendiconti dell'istituto lombardo di sc. e lett.," Milan, 1941-1942, pp. 115-131.
[195] Fichte, *The Vocation of the Scholar*, English translation by A. Carnesecchi.

potentially cosmopolitan society is actually a community in which "a reciprocal action through freedom" shall be exercised through perfecting oneself and the whole society, according to a process of universalization of emancipation that cannot but find in mankind, and therefore in the cosmopolitism, its own most coherent landing point. In society—explains Fichte—each individual wishes to find someone similar to his ideal of man, and for this very reason, when he runs into individuals who may not be at the level of such an ideal, he tries in every way to lead them to it through the work of enhancement and of "moral elevation." In this way then, each one aims at perfecting himself as well as all the others, thus producing a universal "enhancement" of the entire species which leads by that very act to the cosmopolitism of emancipation as its own fundamental projection horizon. This is, needless to say, in direct antithesis with the cosmopolitism of the egoisms imposed by the commercial anarchy (*Anarchie des Handels*) denounced with quivering pathos in *The Closed Commercial State*.[196] Writes Fichte:

> We may therefore say that mutual improvement—improvement of ourselves by the freely admitted action of others upon us, and improvement of others by our reaction upon them as upon free beings—is our vocation in Society.[197]

In this very labor of enhancement of oneself and others (and thus of the whole community as a living and organic totality of individuals who freely act upon themselves and others for their own reciprocal improvement) lies, in Fichte's view, the vocation of man in society, "where the success of one member is the success of all, and the loss of one, a loss to all."[198]

---

[196] J.G. Fichte, *Der geschlossene Handelsstaat*, 1800; tr. it. *Lo Stato commerciale chiuso*, (Milan: Bocca, 1909), p. 70.
[197] J.G. Fichte, *The Vocation of the Scholar*, Lecture II.
[198] Ibid., Lecture III.

From a different perspective, one can claim that the first lecture may find now its own coherent answer: If in this lecture the mission of man is to become man is upheld, namely the uninterrupted self-improvement, now this mission is better determined through the specification that *such labor of perfecting can be realized only in a social form*, in the concrete dimension of the social living. Man's destination is identified, thereon, with the process of emancipation of himself and of the community according to the more and more universal and (asymptotically) closer way to that cosmopolitism that coincides with the entirety of humanity as an undifferentiated and indivisible unity, once again namely as a unique self-conscious subject who takes action in view of his own never-achieved emancipation, in view of "the universal interaction of the whole human race on itself" (*Einwirken des ganzen Menschengeschlechtes auf sich selbst*).[199]

The goal of humanity is always delayed, thereon, only to reactivate the action all over again. As Fichte explains, we are at this time abysmally far away from it, to such an extent that—strictly speaking—we cannot even label ourselves as human beings in a proper sense, since humanity (the becoming man-of man) is the destination of our action.[200] Such a sidereal distance from the aim is understandable because the French Revolution marks the beginning of the so-called age of the "completed sinfulness," as Fichte will uphold somewhere else (even though the expression could easily date back to the *Lectures* on the scholar, given the scathing critique of the cowardice of the present time).

This is an era in which the world turned its back to its social bound in order to consecrate the individual's search for economical profit coherently with the cold logics of the

---

[199] Ibid.

[200] See on this point, Aldo Masullo, *Fichte: l'intersoggettività e l'originario*, p. 166: "Fichte thinks, by once more anticipating Marx, that for a social transformation objectively necessary, it will be finally achieved the end of what is only the prehistory of humanity."

illuminist's thoughts and abstraction that, on the ontological level, unties the parts from the whole and makes them absolute as such, while on the sociopolitical level, it unbinds the individuals from the community and turns them into something absolute like Robesonian individuals. The French Revolution, whilst it had the merit to take down despotism and remove the dominant negative, has not been able to create a world up to its endeavour. The French Revolution destroyed everything and created nothing, being fundamental as much as insufficient, as Fichte highlights in a crucial passage in the following *Speeches to the German Nation*:

> *It is apparent and, I believe, generally granted that the impulse and effort of the age has been seeking to dispel dim feelings and to secure the sole mastery for clearness and knowledge. This effort has been quite successful at least in this, that it has completely revealed the nothingness of the past (das bisherige Nichts vollkommen enthüllt ist). The impulse towards clearness should not be rooted out, nor should dull acquiescence in dim feeling again obtain the mastery. Rather must this impulse be developed still further and introduced into higher spheres (soll nur noch weiter entwickelt und in hohere Kreise eingefuhrt werden), so that when the Nothing has been revealed, the Something, the positive truth that sets up something real, may likewise become manifest.* [201]

Exactly like, in the theoretical field, Kant's first *Critique* had started the "Copernican revolution" without completely unfolding it, so in the practical historical field, the French Revolution has remained an "incomplete process" [202] that has

---

[201] J.G. Fichte, *Addresses at the German Nation*, Third Addresses, Wikisource, 1922.
[202] See Jürgen Habermas, *Die Moderne: ein unvollendetes Projekt*, in Id., *Kleine politische Schriften (I-IV)*, (Frankfurt a.M: Suhrkamp, 1980), pp. 444-464. English translation by A. Carnesecchi.

to be ultimate through re-establishing the *new social and truth-seeking fundamentals up to the times*, able to counterpose the hendiadys of Utilitarianism and Empiricism that rules the era in which—as Cesa has underlined—"Fichte sees the worst elements of the Enlightenment and the reaction against them to converge together—a combination therefore of utilitarian Empiricism and visionary activism, of Enlightenment and Romanticism."[203] From the Revolution has arisen a world that, emptied of transcendence, has surreptitiously elevated Empiricism—and therefore realism of acceptance of the existing reality—to a dominant dimension, choosing as its own philosophy of reference "the worst of all philosophical systems, that of Locke." [204]

The triumph of Utilitarianism and of the abstract principles of the almanac-like intellect of the French encyclopedists has crumbled humanity into a *detached atomistic of loneliness*. Its logical consequence is therefore the overturning of freedom (of the liberation process) of the community in the general subjugation of the singular individuals disconnected from their social context. The individuals are thus submitted to the hetero-directed as well as self-referential process of that unlimited production of value in which is condensed the spirit of the commercial anarchy. Even those who think they are free actually are slaves, as Rousseau teaches us, because—as we have seen—for Fichte one can be free only if everybody is free, namely if the community meant as unitary subject is free.

A particularly sensitive issue upon which Fichte focuses his attention in this second lecture is the one that has already been mentioned before, even though without dwelling on it, of the enhancement of labor that each one—and especially the intellectual—is called to carry out on his fellow men in the always-reiterated attempt to lead them to the ideal of perfection. Does this operation not imply the risk of violence on

---

[203] C. Cesa, *Introduzione a Fichte*, p. 178. English translation by A. Carnesecchi.
[204] J.G. Fichte, *The Charecteristics of the Present Age*, 1806, Wikisource.

the nature of our own counterparts? Do we have any right to try to liberate those who prefer to remain slaves? Fichte, after all, fully agrees with Kant on the matter that man may use as instruments the non-reasonable being but never the reasonable ones. The latter are ends and, as such, they need to be considered and actually treated according to what has been prescribed by one of the *Categorical Imperative's (kategorischer Imperativ's)* formulations. It follows that, for this very reason, the intellectual cannot even force men to become moral, which is the starting point of the labor of self-enhancement and improvement of society, as long as they may not freely and autonomously decide to start such labor. For however paradoxical it could seem, no man has, therefore, the right to force his counterpart to be free: "He may not make any reasonable being either virtuous or wise, against his own will."[205]

The only way out from this question (how to perfect, without any coercion, human beings who, unaware of man's vocation, do not have any intention to start off the difficult journey of self-enhancement) is for the intellectual to use culture as an instrument of "docile persuasion" aimed at making reasonable beings aware (without any coercion) of mankind's goal, as well as of its ontological potentialities, so that they shall, thereon, spontaneously follow the intellectual on the infinite way that leads humanity towards the correspondence to his own genre.

In such a way, the triangular nexus of culture, intellectuals, and society becomes finally clear. By following Fichte's reasoning, the intellectual is the one who makes use of his own knowledge in a social way helping those who are not intellectuals to acquire the awareness of the existence of a goal for humanity and ensure that they may freely take part in the process of mankind's emancipation. The intellectual—this is the corollary—is called to stimulate through culture the praxis of other reasonable beings in such a way that they shall take

---

[205] Fichte, *The Vocation of the Scholar*, Lecture II.

action while being aware of the common goal and let themselves be guided by the intellectual in the gradual process of approaching the destination of man becoming man (in accordance with the genre).

On the sociopolitical level, man's destination in society, as has been outlined so far by Fichte, leads to the consequence—which is certainly worthy of consideration—that the philosopher himself highlights: If all men were able to become perfect, therefore they would all be perfect and *perfectly the same*, to such an extent that they would get to the point of being an absolute and harmonious unity, a totality (*totalitas*) in which the equal freedom of each one would make the equal freedom of everyone possible.

Equality—*equal freedom*—becomes the necessary outcome of mankind's process of emancipation. "The last, highest end of Society, writes Fichte, is the perfect unity and unanimity of all its possible members" (*ist das letzte, höchste Ziel der Gesellschaft völlige Einigkeit und Einmuthigkeit mit allen möglichen Gliedern derselben*).[206]

In the 1798 *Lectures on the Theory of Ethics*, the theme of the perfect unity (*völlige Einigkeit*) will be examined in depth and to a certain extent, radicalized in the thesis according to which, the end of history corresponds to a "communion of saints" (*Gemeinde der Heiligen*). Since it is, once more, an unreachable goal that requires the uninterrupted process of asymptotic approximation, man's true destination in society corresponds with a deeper and deeper social union that becomes more and more internally and externally radical ("to deepen" in the sense that each one perceives it as his own union, and he feels part of it as he increasingly develops mankind's self-consciousness) as more and more human beings become part of it, according to the coordinates of the emancipation's cosmopolitanism recalled before:

---

[206] J.G. Fichte, *The Vocation of the Scholar*, II lecture.

This approximation towards perfect unity and unanimity with all men may be called co-operation (dieses Annahern zur völligen Einigkeit und Einmuthigkeit mit allen Individuen können wir Vereinigung nennen). Thus co-operation, growing ever firmer at its center and ever wider in its circumference, is the true vocation of man in Society.[207]

We return, by following this route, to a theme upon which we have already focused: the social cosmopolitism remains the destination of the process of man's perfecting, the necessary outcome of the acquisition of the self-consciousness and conformity to mankind that together correspond to man's true goal. It is—better to highlight it—a cosmopolitanism completely different compared to the one that the commercial anarchy has generated in its own image, namely the alienated cosmopolitanism of egotisms produced by the scission put in place by the abstract intellect of the Enlightenment. By contrast with the dominant model, Fichte's model is the one of *social cosmopolitanism*, therefore sworn enemy of the individualistic code invoked by the Enlightenment. However, Fichte's model is also the one of *social equality*, and thus opposite to the one which emerged from both commercial anarchy and economy's empowerment, [208] which led the individuals to the condition defined by the young Hegel as "the equality of the irrelevance."

It is Fichte himself who concisely summarizes the theoretical acquisitions of his dissertation by insisting on the never-ending process of improvement meant as the goal of humanity, together with the social perspective, according to which each of us aims at perfecting the others so that the society may gradually emancipate as a whole:

[207] Fichte, *The Vocation of the Scholar*, Lecture II.
[208] See Theodoros Papadopoulos, *Die Theorie des Eigentum bei J.G. Fichte*, (München: Ars Una, 1993).

*We may therefore say that mutual improvement
(gemeinschaftliche Vervollkommnung)—improvement of
ourselves by the freely admitted action of others upon us,
and improvement of others by our reaction upon them as
upon free beings—is our vocation in Society.*[209]

For Fichte, this free development of Society and its
increasingly cosmopolitan system—in order to unfold it—it is
necessary that each member makes the two reciprocally
interconnected instances of giving and receiving his own by
making available to society all that he is endowed with
(knowledge, precautions, instruments, etc.), while at the same
time welcoming with benevolence what society is able to offer
in turn. It is only through this dynamic, characterized by these
two interconnected moments of giving and receiving, that the
universal interaction of the whole human race may fully unfold
itself.[210] As we have seen, this interaction would correspond
with communitarianism on a cosmopolitan basis perfectly
achieved, yet in truth always asymptotically postponed.

In this virtuous attempt at conciliating the two instances of
social particularism and cosmopolitan universalism, traces
blatantly emerge that elsewhere (see Preve) have been defined
as "bourgeoisie's unhappy consciousness" (given by his search
for real universalism taken away by the sinful and alienated
universalism of the algid laws of the Economic Order (*mos
economicus*),[211] of which Fichte, with Hegel and Marx, is a
fully-fledged first class exponent.[212] Philosophy has to lay a
truthful foundation upon which to build a new social bond that
goes beyond the pure commercial nexus to which the abstract
intellect has reduced human relations through the
absolutization of the individual against society.

---

[209] J.G. Fichte, *The Vocation of the Scholar*, II Lecture.
[210] Ibid.
[211] See C. Preve, *Storia dell'etica*, (Pistoia: Petit Plaisance, 2007), p. 90 on. And
this author's work *Minima mercatalia, Filosofia e capitalismo*, pp. 274-288.
[212] "*Mos*" means custom and tradition. (https://latin-dictionary.net/definition/
27301/mos-moris). *Mos economicus* means the "Economic Order."

What is, actually, the fundamental law to which our action in society must be subjected to so that it may comply with the moral law, namely the law that prescribes the constant accordance with ourselves? According to Fichte, the above-mentioned moral law can be effectively determined both in a positive way as well as a negative one. (a) According to the negative determination, we cannot treat others as a means, but always and only as an end, as it follows from the great acquisition of Kant's morality (*Moralität*). Otherwise, we would contradict our social impulse. Society, in fact, corresponds with a free reciprocal action of reasonable beings, with the obvious consequence that, by treating others as mere means, we would by that very fact, (*ipso facto*) annihilate our own freedom: As matter of fact, we would end up being ruled by that utilitarian egoism which—symptomatic of the sinful era—is the irreducible enemy of any ethics that aims at an authentic universalistic level. (b) According to the positive determination, the moral law not only forces us to aim at the inner unity but also to a spiritual unity with society, operating in view of the perfecting of others through education. The culture is thus used as an instrument to lead other reasonable beings to freely cooperate in the emancipative process of the human race.

The ultimate end of Society is, thereon, as it has been recalled several times, the unity of all human beings (the self-consciousness acquisition of the human race which fully understand its own unity), unity that can be achieved only in the case that human perfection on a universal scale is attained. Furthermore, even though the last end would remain unattainable (always relaunched in the future according to the logic of the "evil infinite" stigmatized by Hegel), it is also true that the vocation of man in society is to work with no interruption on the progressive unification of the spirits and their aspirations in the attempt to find a universal and cosmopolitan dimension to a particular community upon which it is based. The means through which one comes to this arrival point is, for Fichte, the same as his *Lecture on The Vocation of Man*: culture of which the intellectual is the guardian and at the same time an active propagator in the social network, therefore making it possible for knowledge to concretely affect the social and political structures. Once more, the eminently practico-critical role of culture as is conceived and practiced by the philosopher emerges in blatant and claimed antithesis with the traditional ways of the scholar, rooted in his "ivory tower" of pure contemplation.

Third Lecture:
On the Distinction of Estates in Society

◆

In this lecture, Fichte tries to outline the role of the intellectual in relation to the sociological problem of the estates (Stände) in which society is structured.[213] The intellectual, as a matter of fact, lives the painful experience of scission because he is, on the universal level, a member of society and at the same time, on the particular level, belongs to a specific estate. What does the intellectual actually need to do if his conscience is split into universal and particular, divided into integral legitimation and radical objection of a world which safeguards him as an estate as well as makes the emancipation of the whole humankind impossible?

The intellectual has a mission that is universalistic yet, nevertheless, contradicted by its particularism—in this case, by his empirical sociological position. As a matter of fact, on the one hand, the intellectual is a guide for society as such, and on the other hand is an exponent of another estate which, at first sight, is the bearer of specific interests that are against the

---

[213] On this matter, see L. Fonnesu, *Diritto, lavoro e "Stände": il modello di società di I.G. Fichte*, in *"Materiali per una storia della cultura giuridica,"* 1985, pp. 51-76.

interests of other estates. How could his mission be universalistic if his social position is particularistic? Is there not perhaps the risk, before this concept existed (*avant la letter*), to become the "intellectual organic to a class or an estate"? Before facing this matter, Fichte focuses his attention on the more general problem of society's stratification into estates, upon which this matter completely depends. The mere fact that such estates actually exist is not enough to justify their existence. It is then necessary to answer to the interrogative regarding the legitimacy of the existence of the estates and with them, of the resulting social inequality to thereafter tackle the difficult problem of the coexistence, within the intellectual estate, of a *universalistic mission* and a *particularistic position*.

Fichte lays down the argument by distinguishing between two different types of inequality: the natural and social type. Whereas the first one is insuppressible, the second one not only can but ought to be overcome. As we have seen, social equality is the destination of social activity, the essential condition necessary for the unification process of mankind to fully unfold. By requesting the perfect development of each member, this necessarily implicates free and equal development of each one.

Let us try to clarify this delicate argumentative passage. Fichte deals with it by directly recalling once again the *Wissenschaftslehre*'s principles of the *not-I*, which have multiple and differentiated natures, and because of that differentiated multiplicity, these produce a prismatic multiplicity of individuals who are also differentiated: namely structurally unequal. The result is, in Fichte's words, "a physical inequality to which we not only have contributed, but which we even cannot remove by our freedom."[214]

Anyway, as has been upheld on several occasion in the previous lectures, the goal of taking action in society consists in the asymptotic approximation to the condition in which one

---

[214] Fichte, *The Vocation of the Scholar*, Lecture III.

may fully correspond to himself, in which everything is in accordance with the active subject and is rationalized by his free transformative praxis. Applied to society, this principle of the *Wissenschaftslehre* dictates that one has to strenuously fight so that each member of society, since he is member of a community, attains the full correspondence with his ontological potentialities. In this way, Fichte posited the moral necessity of a free and uniform development of all of its members as a necessary condition for the enhancement of the whole of humanity. It is then understandable in which sense the ultimate aim of every society coincides for Fichte with "the perfect equality of all of its members" (*die völlige Gleichheit aller ihrer Mitglieder*).[215]

In order for the free and equal development of every single member of society, and therefore of the human race as a whole to actually unfold, the social impulse plays a fundamental role in its two determinations, reciprocally connected, that were mentioned in the previous lecture: (a) The impulse of communicating and giving, namely to transmit to others the knowledge to which we are entitled. (b) The impulse of receiving, welcoming, and metabolizing the knowledge that others will offer to us.

In this way, even though it will not be possible to oppress the natural inequality, on the ontological level the social inequality can and ought to be removed in the moral dimension by a fruitful exchange, according to which each one gives to everyone else what he has and receives what they have to offer, making possible a free and equal development of every member of the community (*Gemeinschaft*).[216] Society ensures, thereon,

---

[215] Ibid.

[216] Compared to the lectures on *The Vocation of the Scholar* (1794), with his *Der geschlossene Handelsstaat* (*The Closed Commercial State*), Fichte's perspective changes by 180 degrees. State is now meant as a place where the individual freedom can actually unfold, and as an organization that has the duty of ensuring work and wellbeing to all of its citizens by regulating production and exchange. Moreover, in a strongly organic perspective, it is claimed that, in order to ensure the political balance, the State must forbid the international commerce (only the knowledge must be common patrimony,

that what individuals did not receive directly from nature, they may receive in a mediated way from the community, which therefore addresses the natural inequality. Society cannot neutralize nature, but it can reduce to zero its effects on the social level.

In a perspective that will return almost unchanged in the pages of *The Closed Trading State* (*Der geschlossene Handelsstaat*), in which the State will ensure the free and equal development of the individual against the unrestrained commercial anarchy, Fichte writes:

Society will gather together the special gifts of every individual member into a common fund for the free use of all, and thus multiply them by the number of those who share their advantages; the deficiencies of each individual will be borne by the community, and will thus be reduced to an infinitely small quantity.[217]

---

therefore, transnational and freely circulating) and, to avoid the phenomenon of accumulation of richness, State must substitute gold and silver with a conventional currency that has value only as a means of exchange. Even though there is no possibility to analytically examine the several reasons that led Fichte to such reorientation, those reasons find overall a coefficient of unity in the changed perspective upon history, in a rethinking not so much of the event of the Revolution as such, rather of the "historical world" that started to develop since the Revolution: A world of unlimited globalization and of triumph of the value of exchange, heir of the "abstract thought" of the Enlightenment, of its "delegitimization of the metaphysics" expectations, of its persistently individualistic code, and its elevation of Utilitarianism as the only possible philosophy. Fichte's reaction must be read especially as a reaction to the underworld that the Revolution made to surface with his proposal of a "closed commercial State" that has at its heart, not the individual, but the supportive human community with its concrete needs, in a completed reestablishment of the hegemony of the political level on the economic one. Without going in depth into the *ingens silva* of the secondary literature on the problem of the State in Fichte, this author only refers to some particularly significative works: K. Hahn, *Staat, Erziehung und Wissenschaft bei J.G. Fichte*, (München: Beck, 1969); G. Duso – G. Rametta (ed. by), *La libertà nella filosofia classica tedesca: politica e filosofia tra Kant, Fichte, Schelling e Hegel*, (Milan: Angeli, 2000); J.C. Goddard et alii (ed. by), *Fichte et la politique*, (Bologna: Polimetrica, 2008); G. Solari, *L'idealismo sociale del Fichte*, in "*Rivista di filosofia*," n. 33 (1942), pp. 141-181; C. Cesa, *Noterelle sul pensiero politico di Fichte*, in "Rivista critica di storia della filosofia," n. 1 (1968), pp. 62-80.

[217] Fichte, *The Vocation of the Scholar*, Lecture III.

This social bond combines society "like in one man" in a supportive manner, in which the individual freedom is not suffocated by the coils of the totality, but finds instead its own warranty in it—the only instance in which it shall be repeated—which is able to stem inequality put in place by nature.[218] This social perspective which is still respectful of the individual expressivity of the singular subject will come back in the 1812 *Doctrine of Right (Rechtslehre)*, wherein "each man moves within the State, but he is not just it. His will is only partially absorbed by the State—for the part to which the State is entitled."[219] After all, the fact that natural inequality cannot be removed, regardless of the efforts put into it, is proved by the fact that the multiplicity of the impulses and inclinations depends on the *not-I* which makes structurally diversified—regardless of the free action of the subject—nature, inclinations, and attitudes.

After all, for Fichte, man finds his specific dimension in the social being and not in nature (which instead lies outside the interests of the philosopher, according to the severe as well as justified accusation made by Shelling as well as Hegel in his *The Difference Between Fichte's and Schelling's Systems of Philosophy (Differenz des Fichteschen und Schellingschen Systems der Philosophie*, 1801). Only in society can man actually take action according to freedom by transforming the existing reality and bending it to his own subjectivity. Nature is nothing but the stage upon which mankind is called to take action, to become compliant with himself by exercising his effort on the resistance that nature counterposes to his freedom. From a different perspective, it can be claimed that for Fichte, the ultimate goal of society is social equality—and thereon equal freedom—of all its members, regardless of their physical inequality which remains insuppressible. In this process, a fundamental role is played, once again, by education, which may affect the social impulse and make the singular

---

[218] Ibid.
[219] *SW*, X, p. 538. English translation by A. Carnesecchi.

individuals acquire the consciousness of this goal which, otherwise, would remain known only to intellectuals as custodians of culture.

In the light of these considerations, the question to be asked is the following: If equality is the destination of the process of humanity's enhancement, how could it unfold when society keeps on being divided into estates to which this equality seems to be the polar opposite? Such an inequality seems, thereon, to deeply contradict the ideal of the complete equality of the members of society, which emerged from the previous lecture, as the result of this compliance with mankind.

To clarify this delicate point, Fichte starts off in the genealogical way and tries to explain why, actually, within society different estates take shape. If one retraces back to the estates' formation with a genealogical outlook, the contradiction is only apparent because of the physical inequality from which different inclinations, capabilities, and interests develop in each individual; each one is called to specialise himself in a sector that is more suitable for him, so that he is able to freely give his contribution to society. The existence of the physical difference is, therefore, that of an organism composed of different parts unified by a common end towards which the components aim because they are part of a unitary social body. The different classes make the development of the human community possible for the self-determination of each individual according to his own capabilities ("it is not the estate that ennobles the subject, rather the subject's unfolding through it"),[220] to then receive from the very same community what the individual requires in order to live and satisfy his own needs. Equality and division in estates not only are not one against the other, but for Fichte, seem to virtuously melt within the organic community thought as a unity: "Thus even from the physical inequality of

---

[220] J.G. Fichte, *The Vocation of the Scholar*, Lecture III. English translation by A. Carnesecchi.

individuals arises a new security for the bond which unites them all in one body."[221]

The estate takes shape as a set of subjects who exert one of the multiple, particular possibilities of objectivations of their own faculties within society. Even though they mostly depend on nature and physical environment, the choice of the estate of belonging must, nevertheless, be free, resulting from the decision of the singular subject who freely unfolds his own nature. For Fichte, society's stratification in estates neither impedes the individual freedom of choice, nor hinders equality's realization—as we have seen—or more precisely, the free and equal development of every member of society and, thereon, of the social community as such. Roberta Picardi significantly wrote:

> *Equality is for Fichte a goal dictated by the supreme rational law of the absolute identity. It is a destination that, however, is unreachable, and towards which to infinitely aim at through the institution of the new inequality represented by the division of society in estates. Such a division does not only seem legitimate but also indirectly appropriate for the individual, since it is the only means by which to contribute the most to the perfecting of mankind.*[222]

The choice of the estate remains free, on the other hand, because it is up to all of us to decide to develop only one of our faculties, namely one of the tendencies that nature established in ourselves, and that we are neither able to leave out of consideration, nor from which we can free ourselves. If the choice of the estate is obligatory, as happens in the feudal world and—even though in a flexible way under the pressure of merely financial coarctation—in the capitalistic world, it is

---

[221] Ibid.

[222] Roberta Picardi, *Il concetto e la storia: la filosofia della storia di Fichte*, (Bologna: Il Mulino, 2009), p. 154. English translation by A. Carnesecchi.

necessary to fight in order to change the establishment and to impose the free determination of the estates accordingly to one's own faculties as well as one's free choices.

After all, for Fichte, to force someone to belong to one estate or to exclude him from another is a disservice to reason and ethics for at least two reasons: First of all, because nobody can know better than the subject himself his own particular inclinations, and consequently nobody is legitimately able to make a choice for him; secondly, to force the nature of a reasonable being and openly go against his decision is to violate the moral law and the assumption of the free development of everyone as a condition for everyone's free enhancement. By forcing the subject to adhere to an estate that otherwise he would not freely choose is to act against his freedom: We wanted a free subject and a "free partner" and we make of him, in a completely opposite way, a passive, unfree instrument.

It is not difficult to grasp between the lines of Fichte's discourse a frontal attack against the old order (*ancien régime*) of society still dominant in the German world, which does not allow the subjects, among other things, to freely choose their own estate of belonging. We must not forget that exactly in 1794, Prussia entered into force *The Prussian Civil Code* (*Preußisches Allgemeines Landrecht*), a very vast work of codification inspired by the grounds of the enlightened despotism which is, nevertheless, still focused on social estates' immobility. By impeding the free choice of estate—explains Fichte—society negates mankind's aim towards free self-development, as well as the development of society as a whole; namely, a precise knowledge of man's attitudes and needs that is able to wisely blend theory with practice in the contemplative dimension as well as the practical one (once more detaching the traditional figure of the learned person).

In such a way, according to Fichte, a society in which everyone is able to choose his own estate of belonging according to the inclination that nature gave him takes shape and, together with the totality (*totalitas*) of the community, this society is able to guarantee an equal development of everyone by equally spreading acquisitions, results, and products that every estate is able to gain. What has been upheld above becomes therefore, truly meaningful: Society can address nature's inequality, even though it is not able to neutralise it (society can just annihilate natural inequality's effects on the social being's level). It becomes, thereon, possible for the free development of humanity, by perfecting each member while perfecting itself, to assert social equality as a remedy to nature's inequality which, insuppressible in its effects, finds in the estates' stratification the most evident appearance.

It is from such a perspective that Fichte can emphatically insist upon the social value of culture, of which the intellectual is the bearer, envisaging a solution to the dilemma from which we started (the ambiguity of a universalistic vocation of a particular estate): Nobody has the right to withdraw from society (according to the scholar's model) and to satisfy, according to a solipsistic-Robesonian scheme, his cultural and individual needs. In particular the intellectual "does not own his knowledge for his own self-interest, but for the benefit of the community."[223] Each one is called upon instead to give an actual contribution to the society of which he is an integral part, since he profoundly owes this to society: It is indeed because of society's work that he has been able to acquire the knowledge that he would like to egoistically and autonomously enjoy. In doing so, the individual—who should be called "scholar"—steals from society, and therefore, from his fellowmen, disowning the world that made possible his cultural formation.

Antithetical if compared to the traditional scholar, the figure of the intellectual spreads his knowledge and, in accordance with it, acts to transform society and to make its enhancement and perfection possible: "Reason will take care that each individual receive indirectly from the hands of

---

[223]J.G. Fichte, *The Vocation of the Scholar*, Lecture III.

society the whole and complete cultivation which he cannot obtain directly from Nature."[224] In this sense, equality as a goal of society is presented on the social level with Fichte's resounding words as a "uniform progress of culture of all individuals" made possible by the active contribution of everybody together with the intellectual as a guide of humanity. [225] Thus, even though among thousands of difficulties, efforts of any kind, and setbacks, the acquisition of the self-consciousness of the entire humanity occurs that becomes more and more self-aware of its ontological potentialities and of its own unity. Along this road, "Society is combined like one man: What the individual could not accomplish by himself, all are enabled to perform by the combined powers of the community" (*Steht die Gesellschaft zusammen, und steht für Einen Mann; was der Einzelne nicht konnte, werden durch vereinte Krafte Alle vermögen*).[226]

The scholars' estate, like any other, is a particular estate. But for the very reason that it is "shaped" by culture, and specifically, by the principles of the Wissenschaftslehre and its universalistic determination (emancipation of the mankind meant as a subject), its particularism crosses its limits to become emancipative universalism. Unlike the traditional scholars' estate (a particular estate devoid of any universal vocation), the estate of the intellectuals can thus become the particular that enables the universal by spreading culture, taking action in society, and persuading, through the docile force of reason the other reasonable beings to act in view of mankind's common goal.

Only in this way, writes Fichte, "the success of one member is the success of all," triggering a "great [human] chain" in which on one side of society, everybody helps each other and freely transmits knowledge, and on the other side in history, the past generations transmit their own acquisitions to the

---

[224] Ibid.
[225] Ibid.
[226] J.G. Fichte, *The Vocation of the Scholar*, Lecture III.

present one, which in turn will leave these as an inheritance to the future generations. [227] Along the road that follows the course of the epochs, which give rhythm to the generations, man becomes eternal, since he accomplishes an exodus from the narrow perimeters of the limited temporality to then arrive to eternity ("with the assumption of this great task, I have also laid hold of Eternity"). [228] With the theme of man's earned eternity, thanks to his vocation, the third lecture ends under the aspect of eternity (*sub specie aeternitatis*) in a Spinozian tone. [229]

---

[227] Ibid.
[228] Ibid.
[229] Ibid.

Fourth Lecture:
The Vocation of the Intellectual

♦

The lecture, inasmuch as it is entirely devoted to the class of the intellectuals and their social mission, is the arrival point of Fichte's meetings upon *The Vocation of the Scholar* marked by—as we have seen—the theoretical passages relating to the destination of man (first lecture), the destination of man in society (second lecture), and the division of society into estates (third lecture). For its part, the fifth lecture is self-standing— later on to be clarified as such—and eccentric, so to speak, compared to the bodies of work of the other four, since it must be considered as a kind of "reaffirmation" of the vocation of man and intellectual in a contrastive comparison with Rousseau's positions, with which Fichte advantageously contended since the *Revolutionary Writings*.

The fourth lecture opens with Fichte's admission of embarrassment, at times, rhetorical, in front of his listeners. How is it possible to publicly and in a scientifically coherent way discuss the intellectual, when the intellectual is both the one who exposes his thesis and the one who listens? It is then necessary from Fichte's perspective to make the objective point of view prevail on the subjective one, however hard it may seem, by trying to outline the greatness and the limits of the intellectual in an honest way and without too many rhetorical devices. After all, as Fichte explains, even if his mission as "guide of humanity" is the most sublime one that can ever be imagined, it also true that the intellectual is called upon to be the most modest of men. Inasmuch as the intellectual exists in the deepest and most transparent of humanity's self-consciousness, he is perfectly aware in a complementary fashion that the goal towards which mankind aims cannot ever be reached, as well as the distance that separates us from being able to call ourselves humans in an authentic way, according to what has been clearly highlighted in the previous lectures.

Once the difficulty for the intellectual to talk about himself has been outlined and overcome, Fichte looks back to the previous lectures, recalling their fundamental theoretical acquisitions, to then ask the question, the answer to which holds the entire meaning of *Some Lectures on The Vocation of the Scholar (Einige Vorlesungen über die Bestimmung des Gelehrten)*. After having clarified that the mission of man is to correspond to his own concept, and therefore to concretely act in society's texture, Fichte explains it is necessary to ask if each man is automatically and spontaneously able to carry out this mission of the equal and uniform emancipation of mankind as such. Whenever the answer is positive, the vocation of the intellectual would be pointless. Each man, in fact, could autonomously and consciously act in view of this objective, with no need for "guides" or "masters."

Anyway, Fichte negatively answers the question, upholding that the individual is neither aware of the mission of himself as a man, nor of society as an organic unity of subjects that reciprocally act according to freedom. For this reason, the actual individual, instead of operating in view of achieving mankind's destination, is constantly exposed to the risk of passivity and lethargy, namely those that Fichte identifies as the two ills that most certainly must be eradicated from the human soul, in coherence with the principles of the

Wissenschaftslehre (action, effort, praxis, etc.). After all, in Fichte's perspective, in order for the individual to proceed along the infinite way that leads him to correspond with his own concept, it is not even sufficient to pinpoint his imperfections and mistakes, since the one who criticizes without taking the responsibility of perfecting the one who is criticized is actually a wrongdoer.

It is exactly in this difficult task of glacial *critique of the actuality* (and therefore also of the individuals in their actual situations) together with *concrete praxis aimed at transforming the whole society* by accompanying it in the constant effort towards perfection, that the intellectual has to be identified in his synergetic balance between *critical theory* and *transformative praxis* directed to the universal emancipation. His presence and action are justified because the individuals, on their own, would not be able to travel the road of emancipative enhancement, and they would easily give up to the adjustment (*anpassung*) to the inactive system and its balance of power. The intellectual, therefore is called upon to—and herein lies his specific vocation—look after humanity, to educate it, to make it acquire self-consciousness and consciousness of its mission (the asymptotic process of complying with mankind), to guide it in the constant overcoming of obstacles that society meets on its long and rough path.

The intellectual—as was partially found above—employs his most elevated cultural knowledge to educate other men so that, finally aware of humanity's mission, they could give their contribution in a free and active way. In such a way, once more the eminently social, practical, and political vocation of the scholar it is reasserted. "The Scholar [meant as intellectual] is destined in a peculiar manner for society; his class, more than any other, exists only through society and for society."[230] The scholar is called upon to virtuously unify the purely theoretical

---

[230] J.G. Fichte, *The Vocation of the Scholar*, Lecture IV.

knowledge (*philosophy*) with the empirical one (*history*), seeking a fruitful synthesis between the two (*historical-philosophical knowledge*). More precisely, the intellectual must first of all have a philosophical knowledge of humanity's needs in order to satisfy them, and secondly, a historical knowledge that makes him aware of the past, namely of the empirical data that shows evidence of the progress of humanity as it happens, thanks to the intellectual's concrete action as a teacher of mankind. [231] It should be noticed that in *The Closed Commercial State*, Fichte will revisit the idea of the nexus between philosophy and history by developing a conception for which philosophy determines the rational state (*Vernunftstaat*), and then history enables a realistic analysis of the political conditions of the present and the past.

The theme of the fundamental correlation between philosophy and history is codified by Fichte here as one of the core reasons of Idealism—the temporality as the foundation for being (*Seinsgrund*)—and can be found, even though differently unfolded, in Hegel. The truth, given that it cannot be reduced to historicity, does not unfold itself on the level of historical becoming, as "becoming of the true" in the ontological chronicle prospective of Hegel's *The Phenomenology of Spirit* (*Phänomenologie des Geistes*):

> *The True is the whole, but the whole is nothing other than the essence consummating itself through its development. Of the Absolute it must be said that it is essentially a result, that only in the end is it what it truly is...*[232]

---

[231] Cristoph Asmuth, *Metaphysik und Historie bei J.G. Fichte*, in "*Fichte-Studien,*" n. 23 (2003), pp. 145-158.

[232] GW.F. Hegel, *The Phenomenology of the Spirit*, trans. by A.V. Miller, (USA: Oxford University Press, 1977), p. 11. In determining the True as a result, and thereon as a process of becoming-of-the True, is enclosed the secret of Hegel's temporal ontology. In a perspective in which the truth has as a father, Eternity, and as a mother, Time, the philosopher is called, according to Hegel, to consider his own historical time and grasp from it what is true and eternal by judging it according to criteria that cannot be uniquely withdrawn by historicity. Inasmuch as history is nothing but the unfolding of the Idea *sub specie*

Namely, this is a process of the unfolding of self-consciousness
and overcoming all of the obstacles between humanity and its
full compliance with itself:[233]

---

temporis "History is a conscious self-mediating process—Spirit emptied out
into Time *(fällt die Entwicklung der Geschichte in die Zeit)*." "World history" is
the history of the moral unfolding of the Truth of the Idea, as "history of
philosophy" is the process of the unfolding of the truth caught in the thoughts
of the "heroes" of the thinking reason who belong to the Western canon. (Id.,
Lezioni sulla storia della filosofia, ed. by R. Bordoli, p. 609). Here comes Hegel's
thesis regarding the coincidence between philosophy and its history, a thesis
centered upon the belief that the occurring of different philosophical systems
coincides, even though in a flexible fashion, with the occuring of the conceptual
determinations of the Idea that unfolds throughout time, of the totality that
articulates in a rich series of degrees and moments in a temporal perspective.
According to what has been specified in the *Enzyklopädie* (§ 13), "in the
philosophies that manifest and appear to be different, the history of philosophy
shows, on the one hand, that there is only one philosophy in different stages of
its development *(nur eine Philosophie auf verschiedenen Ausbildungs-Stufen
auf)*, and on the other hand, that the specific principles which are the bases of
a given philosophical system are nothing but branches belonging to a whole."
(Id. d., *Enzyklopädie der philosophischen Wissenschaften im Grundrisse*, 1830;
trans in Italian by E. Cicero, *Enciclopedia delle scienze filosofiche in
compendio*, Milan: Bompiani, 2000, p. 119, English translation by A.
Carnesecchi.). Since the "history of the world is, in general terms, the unfolding
of the Spirit through time, as well as the Idea which unfolds as Nature through
space," it follows that our own present time marks the highest point of this
process, the result of the idea's millennial journey. Therefore, in order to be
able to judge the totality, one needs to look at it. "Philosophy is completely
identical to the Spirit of its own time. It is not superior to it, but it is its
conscience; the knowledge of what is substantial is the thinking knowledge
that characterizes an epoch. Seemingly, an individual is not superior to his
own time, as each man is son of his own time. What is substantial in a given
time is the essence of the individual who manifests it in the manner that is
peculiar to him. It is worthless to stand on tiptoe to be able to see further our
time's horizon. It is not possible to jump outside our time, as well as it is not
possible to take off our own skin," ibid., p. 27 (English translation by A.
Carnesecchi.). Upon the nexus between Truth and Time in Hegel, see H.
Marcuse, *Hegels Ontologie und die Grundlegung einer Theorie der
Geschichtlikeit*, 1932; Italian trans. by di E. Arnaud, *L'ontologia di Hegel e la
fondazione di una teoria della storicità*, (Florence: La Nuova Italia, 1969); G.
Tagliavia, *La storia come fenomenologia dell''assoluto in Hegel*, (Palermo:
L''Epos, 1995); C.J. Bauer, *Das Geheimnis aller Bewegung ist ihr Zweck.
Geschichtsphilosophie bei Hegel und Droysen*, (Hamburg: Felix Meiner Verlag,
2001); F. Biasutti, *Il problema della storia nella filosofia di Hegel*, (Padoa:
CLEUP, 1999); J. McCarney, Hegel on History, (London: Routledge, 2000).
[233] See Ives Radrizzani, *Quelques réflexion sur le statut de l'histoire dans le
système fichtéen*, in "*Revue de theologie et de philosophie*," 1991, pp. 293-304. I.
Radrizzani et alii, *La philosophie de l'histoire chez Fichte*, (Paris: Colin, 1996).

*The ultimate purpose of each man is the full compliance
with himself—and, in order to achieve such a condition—
the perfect compliance of all external actualities with
himself through the necessary and practical notions of
actuality, notions that lie in him (that is to say those
notions that determine the way in which the external
actualities should be).*[234]

In regard to the intellectual, no doubt he can completely
overlook historicity to gauge how far mankind has come (that
is, anyway, a historical process), namely to fix *a priori* the goal
of gradual approximation of compliance to the genre. However,
he cannot overlook the historical level in order to actually
understand to which degree of development humanity has
come so far or, from a different perspective, how far the
unfolding of the truth has come at the present time.

The historical knowledge is therefore, fundamental as well
as insufficient. As already clarified in the *Contribution*,
historical knowledge does not end in itself, but is functional to
the philosophical knowledge that is, by its very nature,
inextricably historical according to a theme that will come back
later on in the *Characteristics of the Present Age* even though
differently unfolded. It has been significantly passed down that
Fichte preferred counting peas rather than studying history as
a sequence of facts.[235] By unifying these two determinations
(historical and philosophical), the intellectual can assert a
knowledge of a different kind, the *historical-philosophical* one,
namely—as has been said already—*knowledge of the True in
its unbreakable link with historicity*. The intellectual has,
therefore, to acquire truth in its historical dimension, different
from historicity, by meaning history as a place of

---

[234] J.G. Fichte, *The Vocation of the Scholar*, IV lecture. English translation by
A. Carnesecchi.

[235] J.G. Fichte *im Gespräch. Berichte der Zeitgenossen*, ed. by E. Fuchs in
collaboration with R. Lauth – W. Schieche, 6 voll., Stuttgart/Bad Cannstatt
1978-1992, I, p. 375.

"becoming-true-of the truth," that is the spatiotemporal actualization of the truth. The logical-ontological level of the latter which still maintains a transcendental character and which cannot be reduced to the historical dimension (a historicity without any transcendental sympathy would be nihilistic) does not exist without a necessary correlation with historicity, under the form of time unfolding (in a transcendentalism properly based upon history and not historicity).

Only the intellectual, explains Fichte, is able to develop a holistic and praxis-oriented knowledge: "...but not every individual must attempt to grasp the whole extent of human learning in all these three forms of knowledge." [236] The individual can certainly be a learned person, maybe in the traditional form of the scholar, because he is able to form himself in each of the three sectors outlined before; however, he will not be able to assert the holistic perspective that only the intellectual is able to mature. Because of this "three-dimensional" knowledge (philosophical, historical, and historical-philosophical) the intellectual can carry out his never-ending mission towards his constant perfecting.

...and hence arises the true vocation of the scholar [here meant as the intellectual]; the most widely extended survey of the actual advancement of the human race in general, and the steadfast promotion of that advancement.[237]

Unlike the majority of the chronosophical perspectives of seventeenth and eighteenth century philosophy of history (*Geschichtsphilosophie*), in Fichte there is not an "automatism of history." Progress and emancipation are never guaranteed but, in order to fully unfold, they need the Kantian infinite

---

[236] J.G. Fichte, *The Vocation of the Scholar*, IV lecture.
[237] Ibid.

"army of efforts" (*Heer von Muhseligkeiten*),[238] that lies in the intellectual who, thanks to culture of which he is the bearer,[239] can promote and guide towards the right direction.[240]

After all, the true problem of the philosophical consideration of history invoked by Fichte—in the 1794 lectures but then also in the *Characteristics of the Present Age* and in other writings devoted to this matter—can be summarized as the attempt to harmonise the universal law of development *a priori* of a universal plan, (*Weltplan*), with the freedom of human action (always coherently within the structure of *Wissenschaftslehre*). This is possible by looking for the:

> ...*compatibility between the need of finding a rational law underlying the course of history—with a referral to a cosmic plan or providence—and the need to preserve intact the role of human freedom in the implementation of this process.*[241]

That the dimension of freedom of action is a condition of a universal plan for unfolding which never ceases is demonstrated by the fact that, still late in *The Doctrine of the State* (*Die Staatslehre*, 1813), Fichte will resolutely claim that historical accidents are not inferable since they are the result of free human praxis.[242]

Inasmuch as the intellectual has to guard the effective progress of humanity, more than any other man he has the duty to progress and make an effort, namely to be morally the

---

[238] I. Kant, *Idee zu einer allgemeinen Geschichte in weltbürgerlicher Absicht*, 1784; Italian translation, *Idea per una storia universal dal punto di vista cosmopolitico*, in Id., *Scritti di storia, politica e diritto*, p. 32.

[239] See H. Schüttler, *Freiheit als Prinzip der Ge schichte: die Konstitution des Prinzips der Geschichte [...] nach J.G. Fichtes Wissenschaftslehre*, (Würzburg: Königshausen und Neumann, 1984), pp. 65.

[240] See R. Picardi, *Il concetto e la storia: la filosofia della storia di Fichte*, p. 189 on.

[241] Ibid., p. 73. English translation by A. Carnesecchi.

[242] *SW*, IV, pp. 458-459.

most righteous man of his time. Using Fichte's words, "he ought to exhibit in himself the highest grade of moral culture then possible."[243] Above all, he must always direct his gaze towards the "not-yet," conceiving as merely temporary any actual profit. If the acquisitions achieved time after time were considered as ultimate goals, the effort aimed at infinite perfecting would burn out and, with it, laziness and inactivity would triumph again.

There is an aspect which Fichte emphatically insists upon, and upon which it is good to focus: The fact that the intellectual is the most righteous man of his time and one who puts his culture constantly at the service of all reasonable beings in society, does not mean that he gives without receiving, as this is alien to that fundamental dialectic of giving and receiving that characterizes humanity's social essence. Nobody indeed, explains Fichte, is so ignorant as to not be able to learn or teach something. Consequently, also the most humble and illiterate man will be able to teach something even to the intellectual, thus revealing his own indispensability for the socio-communitarian process of mankind's emancipation. It follows that this intellectual, despite how cultured he may be, is always able to learn from other reasonable beings in a society. Moreover, "He should at all times maintain this receptivity by means of new acquirements, and endeavour to preserve himself from a growing insensibility to foreign opinions and modes of thought" (otherwise there would be the risk to fall once again into the profile of the traditional scholar).[244]

By following the unfolding of Fichte's reasoning, one may wonder at this point how the intellectual actually does spread culture socially (and what is the dissemination of culture). He is the "master of humanity" and "educator of mankind" because in every time and place, he leads his fellowmen to acknowledge themselves as part of a whole, as well as remain oriented towards their constant perfecting and being constantly mindful

[243] J.G. Fichte, *The Vocation of the Scholar*, IV lecture.
[244] Ibid.

of the "not-yet" that means the never-ending overcoming of the existing reality.

In this way, Fichte goes against any elitist theory of culture upon which the traditional figure of the scholar was based; how, will be outlined by Schelling himself. The convergence of Hegel's with Fichte's perspective is blatant on this matter, and in this common stance against the developments of Schelling's thought finds its expressive horizon. "The intellectual intuition" codified by Schelling—very different from the one accepted by Fichte—implies a *gnoseological aristocraticism* for which the authentic philosophical truth, the knowledge of the absolute, is available only to few (along with the emphasization of the role of the "genius"). [245] It is well-known that Hegel, defender of "democratic gnoseology" (Lukács) will harshly target Schelling's stance moved by the two-fold intention of safeguarding the scientificity of philosophy against Schelling's irrationalism, as well as maintaining its availability to everyone (without having, for this reason, either to give up on expository accuracy, or on the "effort of the concept"). Hegel will write:

Philosophy as science of reason, because of its universal essence, is indeed according to its own nature for all. Not everyone comes to it, but this is not the matter, as not all men become princes. What makes [one] sick about [the] fact that some men are above others is only the claim that they are different by nature, they belong to another species.[246]

The lectures on *The Vocation of the Scholar* are themselves based on a similar democratic gnoseology, not only because they thematize the nexus between giving and receiving which

---

[245] See A. Philonenko, *La liberté humaine dans la philosophie de Fichte*, pp. 77-95.

[246] Karl Rosenkranz, *Hegels Leben*, Berlin 1844, p. 186. English translation by A. Carnesecchi.

implies the absolute reciprocity by means of which the scholar ("master of mankind") is called to teach the not-yet-scholar or the scholar-to be and moreover, to learn from him. However, also in an even more decisive way, the very aim of humanity for Fichte coincides with its free development in all of its parts, so that each member will have to acquire in the end that specific cultural education that will make possible "a uniform progress of culture in all individual men,"[247] as well as "for the equal distribution of the culture thus acquired among the individual members of society."[248]

In *Philosophy of Masonry* (*Philosophie der Maurerei*) of 1802, the text that contains Fichte's conferences at the Masonic Lodge of Berlin, the cornerstone of the thesis is that within society there is a set of specific educations (*Bildungen*) which, thanks to Masonry's operations will become one unique *Education for Moral Freedom*, (*Bildung zur sittlichen Freiheit*), and as Fichte qualifies it, harmoniously pursued by all as one body. As De Pascale suggested, "whatever Fichte may think of a 'genius,'...what he is interested in the most is the perfecting of society overall."[249] This thesis, after all, is proved by some of Fichte's unequivocal claims, like the one according to which "the attitude toward philosophy, namely a philosophical stance, is an ability that belongs to all men,"[250] or, again, "reason is common to everyone and it is the same in all reasonable beings."[251]

As already said, in order to carry out this duty of educator and guide of mankind, the intellectual is called upon to use his own culture in order to show his own fellowmen, with the docile strength of reason, humanity's mission in its actual stage of progress. Consequently, he cannot resort to coercive means or deceits. If he actually resorted to coercive means, then he

---

[247] J.G. Fichte, *The Vocation of the Scholar*, III lecture.
[248] Ibid.
[249] C. De Pascale, *Etica e diritto. La filosofia pratica di Fichte e le sue ascendenze kantiane*, p. 80. English translation by A. Carnesecchi.
[250] *NS*, p. 3. English translation by A. Carnesecchi.
[251] J.G. Fichte, *Werke. Auswahl in sechs Bänden*, III, p. 91.

would violate the freedom of his fellowmen, finding himself acting against the principles of the perfecting of mankind. Equally, if he used deceitful expedients and deceptions, then he would treat his fellowmen as mere means and not like free individuals, acting once again against the principles and the aims of humanity. At the end, it is the same reason for which, as we have seen in the previous lecture, nobody has the right to place an individual in a given estate without having prior consent and freedom to choose his social collocation. Such a gesture would end up "atrophying" a member of society and at the same time, would stress this natural inequality that society must instead make uninfluential.

The intellectual's duty as a guide of mankind is made even more difficult—Fichte points out—because of the "emasculated and weak" [252] time in which humanity finds itself living, tending to indistinctively liquidate as "fanaticism" (*Schwärmerei*) all that is against it and all that it is not able to elevate.[253] The present time, as progenitor of the decomposing logic of the abstract intellect and its irresistible and univocal passion for what is useful—in which Fichte sees what he will later call "the accomplished sinfulness"—only glorifies empiricism and therefore, the world as it actually is by demonizing every educational ideal and every concrete attempt to found an ethical community taken away from the ice-cold laws of *mos econimicus*. In open contrast with his time and perennially unconciliated with the existing reality, the intellectual is urged by truth, of which he is the minister and in the name of which he is also ready to sacrifice his own life, to act within and for society. With this very declaration of courage and of opposition against the "spirit of time" ends the fourth lecture.

---

[252] J.G. Fichte, *The Vocation of the Scholar.*
[253] See G. Florschütz, *Mystik und Aufklärung: Kant, Swedenborg und Fichte*, in *"Fichte-Studien,"* n. 21 (2003), pp. 89-107.

Fifth Lecture:

Examination of Rousseau's Doctrines Concerning the Influence of Art and Science on the Wellbeing of Man

♦

This lecture, as disclosed before, is eccentric compared to the other four, since it is an attempt to value what it has been upholding through the contrastive comparison with Rousseau's theses. Compared to Fichte's, Rousseau's theses converge for what concerns their diagnosis, but they are in contrast for what concerns their therapy. Fichte does not examine Rousseau's thought of *The Social Contract* (*Contrat Social*, 1762) from which he took inspiration for writing his *Contribution*, but he focuses on the *Discourse on the Arts and Sciences* (*Discours sur les sciences et les arts*, 1750). His lecture opens with the problematization of the philosophical truth, by revealing once more how, for one side, the *Wissenschaftslehre* is the solid foundation of his thought and essential to understanding the real extent of the 1794 lectures on the intellectual. It is only by starting from such a stable and irrefutable basis, explains Fichte, that it becomes possible to proceed with the system of the truth, unmasking the figures of the falsehood which, from time to time are met along the way, "as truth is a touchstone both of the truth itself and of falsehood" (*verum index sui et falsi*).[254]

Nevertheless—argues the thinker from Rammenau—it can be extremely useful to challenge some erroneous and misleading stance because such a confrontation allows bringing out the truth via contrastive rhetoric. It is in a similar perspective that, in this fifth lecture, Fichte chooses to focus on Rousseau's theses. Rousseau, actually draws up a bright critique of the present time, glimpsing in it some of the traits of rampant egoism, and accurately finding its cause in the antisocial and abstract character of Enlightened Reason ("With deep indignation he rebuked his Age"), but offers a solution completely unsatisfactory for the reasons that shall be highlighted right away. [255] Instead of individuating in the transformative praxis as a possible escape from the ills of the present age, Rousseau offers an anachronistic and sterile throwback to the original condition crystalized in the metaphor of the "state of nature," thus paralysing the effort of the praxis through nostalgia that inevitably leads to resignation. It is exactly in this sense that, in Fichte's literature, the exactness of Rousseau's diagnosis aporetically coexists with the complete failure of the therapy. Fichte's intent is clear and he sharply explains it: "We shall understand Rousseau better than he understood himself, and will shall discover him to be in perfect harmony with himself and with us."[256]

From Fichte's point of view, Rousseau draws from his correct diagnosis a totally misleading solution, since he develops the certainty—which is completely illegitimate—that

---

[254] The paradox is well known, according to which the philosophical term "nihilism" appears for the first time presumably in Jacobi who, in 1799, uses it for describing Fichte's idealism: "In truth, my dear Fichte, it does not really bother me if you Sir, or whoever, want to call chimerism what I counterpose to idealism to which I move the reprimand of nihilism." F.H. Jacobi, Werke, Leipzig, III, 1816, p. 44). See M.A. Gillespie, *Nihilism before Nietzsche*, (Chicago: The University of Chicago Press, 1995); A. Iacovacci, *Idealismo e Nichilismo. La lettera di Jacobi a Fichte*, (Padoa: CEDAM, 1992).
[255] J.G. Fichte, *The Vocation of the Scholar*, V lecture.
[256] Ibid.

progress as such is the origin of every evil. The fact that progress made possible the present time's evil (utilitarianism, egoism, metaphysical agnosticism, sceptical relativism, and indifference) is erroneously considered a proof of the corruption linked to the progress and the perfecting of mankind. The paradox folded into Rousseau's reasoning is, after all, reinforced by the fact that the solution is based on the need to remove culture—meant as cause of evil—to go back to the Golden Age (*saturnia regna*, of the "noble savage" as well as on the awareness that such a "return to the past" is entirely impracticable. Since the beginning, Rousseau's project is known to be a failure, determining as an inevitable consequence the acceptance of the existing reality, therefore considered non-transcending. Then, here comes Rousseau's profoundly unhappy character, aware of the evil and at the same time, of the fact that it is incurable.

One must not miss out on how Fichte largely deforms Rousseau's thought, misunderstanding some of the decisive points (first of all the conception of the "state of nature") or, more likely bending it to his use (*ad usum sui*), and therefore creating a profile perfectly functional to his own critique. Leaving out the misunderstandings and the errors—quirky at times—made by Fichte in outlining Rousseau's position, let us dwell upon those that, for Fichte, are Rousseau's flaws and prominences.[257] If progress coincides with regression, it follows that it is historically impracticable. Rousseau's solution is, in this respect, totally ruinous as such, and actually neutralises his critical strength (the invective against the present ends up being neutralized by the correlate admission of the impossibility to transcend the actual system): "To stand aloof and lament over the corruption of man, without stretching forth a hand to diminish it (explains Fichte) is weak

[257] See R. Schottky, *Das Problem der Gewalteiligung bei Rousseau und Fichte*, in "*Daimon. Revista de filosofia*," n. 9 (1994), pp. 289-322; W. Janke, *Entgegensetzungen. Studien zu Fichte-Konfrontationen von Rousseau bis Kierkegaard*, (Amsterdam: Rodopi, 1994).

effeminacy."[258] Nevertheless, Rousseau's thought hosts hints of truth that cannot be liquidated or even scaled down. Among those, his diagnosis of his time's sinfulness is the most relevant, and Fichte himself does not hesitate to metabolize it, even though by envisioning—as will be said right away—such a declination that will trigger an actual program of rejuvenation of the world through praxis.

"His actions (writes Fichte about Rousseau) stand in opposition to his principles" because humanity's emancipation and liberation from all of its present-time ills, towards which Rousseau aims, are possible only through culture and praxis pointed towards the future, certainly not through the inertia of those who passively observe the state of things dreaming of a past definitely gone.[259] In particular, in front of the deviations of his time, "Rousseau was now incapable of seeing anything but the object which had called it forth," without being actually able to find a therapy or a strategy of practical reaction.[260]

The very concept of culture as thought by Rousseau is for Fichte deeply problematic: Education and culture are considered by Fichte to be the basis of his project for mankind's emancipation, guided by the knowledge of the intellectuals and their ability to reprogram the existing reality's syntax as well as reorganise the other rational beings," as action on the basis of their cultural formation. Rousseau's belief that culture is the origin of all ills of the present time was summed up by Fichte with the following expression: "The advancement of culture is the sole cause of all human depravity." This would keep in check Fichte's project as well as individuate in the intellectual estate the origin of the present sinfulness and not its possible remedy.[261] From Fichte's point of view, far from being the cause of every evil, culture is the source of the possible resilience to the ills and emancipation of mankind.

---

[258] Fichte, *The Vocation of the Scholar*, V lecture.
[259] Ibid.
[260] Ibid.
[261] Ibid.

Moreover, Rousseau's protest remains individual and does not urge other reasonable beings to act and concretely organize in view of the transformation of the existing reality—in view of the future compliance between the object and the subject. Because Rousseau's protest lacks social value, it is therefore condemned to be ineffective against the individual protest, which is known to be a failure since the beginning, and for this very reason gives up on any transformative passion.

Anyway, in Rousseau's diagnosis, there is another aspect that Fichte celebrates and does not hesitate to make his own: The critique of the intellectuals of his time who, instead of taking up their vocation as guides of humanity in view of their perfecting, integrally adhere to the system, to the egoism, to the utilitarianism, to the relativistic and metaphysically agnostic scepticism, and to the symbolic reproduction of the morphology of the world. In the present case, for Fichte, the intellectuals of the Enlightenment galaxy who had a precise critical and transformative function tend irremediably to align with the power, becoming the "guard dogs" of the system.

Once more, in Rousseau's analysis from the correct diagnosis originates a misleading therapy: As a fact, from the right verification with regard to the corruption of the intellectuals of the present time, the Genevan thinker draws the unfounded consequence that intellectuals and culture as such are responsible for every evil of the past, present, and future. In this way, he neutralizes the possibility of a practical overcoming of the contradiction that has been diagnosed, and this makes his own exact critical diagnosis totally ineffective.

As Rousseau teaches us that the intellectuals of the present time are in large part directly responsible for the time's sinfulness, for Fichte this is an irrefutable, matter-of-fact discussion on which he closes the fourth lesson. On the symbolic and cultural level, there are intellectuals who defend the widespread lethal bond between empiricism and sensualism—namely that blind faith in the senses and the consequent opposition to reason—in the givenness (empiricism) of existing reality, and in the consequent removal of every "must-be" that points at the future. "How to enjoy as much as possible and to do as little as possible," is how Fichte summoned up the unbridled ills of the present time. [262] Whenever it shall be possible to go back to the "state of nature," according to Rousseau's vague hopes, both sensualism and empiricism would certainly disappear, and even the historically acquired human self-consciousness and reason—substituted by the original harmonious and non-egoistical sensuality—would vanish away.

Once more, however, there is some truth in Rousseau's discourse, especially for what concerns his explicit thematization of the natural—sociable and communitarian—character of man. Man, as such, is sociable and common-good oriented. His actual egoism and wickedness are historically determined and more precisely connected with the actual structure of society as it has been shaped throughout its historical unfolding. By embracing Rousseau's anthropology—as well as Aristotle's anthropology as seen in the second lecture—of man as a social, communitarian, and political animal, Fichte rejects Hobbes' anthropology crystalized by Fichte in the form of the "unsociable sociability"[263] of "a man is wolf to another man" (*homo homini lupus*), as, however, he already referred to in his *Contribution*:

> *One needs to reject that ancient and faulty representation of man's state of nature: that war of all against all that there should rightfully be; that right of the strongest who should rule this Earth…. I do know that you always recall*

---

[262] Ibid.

[263] See I. Kant, *Idea per una storia universale dal punto di vista cosmopolitico*, p. 33. The expression *"ungesellige Geselligkeit"* is used by Kant to stress humans' tendency to unite (sociability) linked to the opposite tendency to divide, to that hostility anthropologically founded on Hobbes' premises (unsociability). The "unsociable sociability" finds its most effective expression in the global market, in which the world sociability is founded upon a radically egoistical and antisocial basis.

> *the original wickedness of man, of which, however, I cannot convince myself.*[264]

Made up by a radical "future-centrism," a very extraordinary valuation of the future (*extraordinaire valorisation de l'avenir,* as Philonenko qualified it), [265] through Rousseau, Fichte's ontology of praxis diagnoses the present-time ills, and at the same time, by moving further from Rousseau's perspective, offers to cure them through the human social praxis aimed at the future as a place of overcoming the present contradictions. The glacial critique of existence is thus based upon the transformative praxis, animating it as well as finding in it its own natural fulfillment in that "future-centered" tension that is for Fichte, the mark of man's being in the world: "In the anticipation of the future lies the true character of humanity" (*in der Aussicht in die Zukunft liegt der wahre Charakter der Menschheit*).[266]

By varying the lexicon of Kant's first *Critique,* for Fichte the critique without praxis is empty and the praxis without critique is blind. The intellectual, since he is called to safeguard the progresses and the emancipative processes of mankind, must constantly have his eyes turned to the future, considering every acquisition as functional to future destination, according to the theme at the center of the fourth lecture.

For what has been upheld until now, it follows that the Golden Age that Rousseau has incautiously projected back into the past of an original "state of nature" must instead be placed, prospectively, into the dimension of the future made possible by the praxis of a humanity reunited and guided by the intellectuals. [267] With Fichte's words: "Thus what Rousseau, under the name of the state of nature, and these poets, under

---

[264] J.G. Fichte, *Contributo per rettificare i giudizi del pubblico sulla Rivoluzione francese,* pp. 142-143, English translation by A. Carnesecchi.

[265] A. Philonenko, *La liberté humaine dans la philosophie de Fichte,* p. 71.

[266] Fichte, *The Vocation of the Scholar,* V lecture.

[267] A similar "future-centered" tone is also traceable in Fichte's *Vocation of Man.*

the title of the Golden Age, place behind us, lies actually before us." [268] Hence, culture, thanks to the intellectuals as its legitimate bearers and diffusers, must allow us to emancipate in the present time, overcoming it in the direction of the future. There is not any historical law that makes necessary this passage; that can happen only thanks to the actual praxis of a humanity that is both self-conscious and conscious of its own objectives, ontologically possible and morally necessary.

In the light of what has been said while retracing Fichte's dissertation, the reservations raised by Fichte in regard to Rousseau's can essentially be reduced to two: (a) "The ease of life" upon which he fantasized and considered as impossible (since the return to the state of nature is impracticable) will be possible in the future through the practical action of humanity guided by the intellectual. (b) Rousseau's solution ends up annihilating every actual instance of praxis, action, and effort, wrongfully projecting humanity into that inertia that is, in and of itself, one of the most pernicious ills of the present, coinciding, as a matter of fact, with the fully unfolded immorality (in this, Rousseau remains a son of his time (*volens nolens*).

Especially from this last aspect, according to Fichte, arises the weakness of Rousseau's solution. Even though this solution has the merit of waking us up from the "dogmatic sleep" of the lazy, acritical acceptance of the existing reality, it ends up avoiding the start of the journey of the praxis aimed at overcoming the present in view of the future, in an unforgivable undervaluation of mankind and of his capability to concretely transform reality. In this sense, as Fichte writes, Rousseau "felt strongly the miseries of mankind, but he was far less conscious of his own power to remedy them."[269]

Because he is not able to transform his own incompatibility with the present in practico-transformative energy, Rousseau remains, from Fichte's point of view, "the man of passive

---

[268] Fichte, *The Vocation of the Scholar*, V Lecture.
[269] Ibid.

sensibility, not at the same time of proper active resistance to its power." [270] In him is completely missing "the militant optimism" that looks at the future and acts in its name: He stops at the monotony of the "it-is-so," in which he deciphers with critical accuracy the respective limitations for which he is not able to outline a concrete solution, because he has not faith in humanity, culture, and praxis. Fichte writes, "Thus Rousseau throughout depicted Reason *at peace*, but not *in strife*; he weakened Sense instead of strengthening Reason.*"*[271]

It is with an exhortation to the transformative praxis that the fifth lecture ends, the conclusion of which undoubtedly sounds as an exhortation aimed at the listeners so that they themselves take on, like Fichte, the role of the intellectual to guide humanity towards the infinite process of emancipation and enhancement: "Act! Act!—it is to that end we are here."[272]

The Vocation of the Scholar, no less than the *Wissenschaftslehre* in all its versions, reminds us that "the being-according-to the possibility" is the fabric on which reality is woven—the existing reality unfolds when it has been possible (*esse sequitur posse*)—and as a consequence, the opportunity "to be-different-from-how-one-is" unfolds, to reprogram the syntax of the world even when, as is the case currently, it is ubiquitously declared unchangeable (in an unexpected triumph of the *not-I* on the *I*).[273]

More than ever, in the figurative desert landscape of this postmetaphysic and postmodern time, the worst of mankind's tendencies unfold and are condemned with rigorous passion by Fichte. The practical change and the dimension of the future seem to be frozen under the layer of the eternal present. Fichte's thought, and in the this case his practical and

---

[270] Ibid.
[271] Ibid.
[272] Ibid.
[273] See this author's *Philosophy and Hope, Bloch and Löwith interpreters of Marx*, (Mimesis International, 2017), as well as Lukács, *Zur Ontologie des gesellschaftlichen Seins*, 1972; tr. It. ed by A. Scarponi, *Per l'ontologia dell'essere sociale*, (Rome: Editori Riuniti, 1976), 2 vol. out of three.

futurological vocation delivered in the pages of the *Bestimmung Gelehrter*, cannot but "provoke," from Latin *"provocare,"* that is, literally to call us out" from hiding behind the sterile absolutism of impartiality (*Wertfreiheit*), impelling us to "come out of the closet" and openly take a position with regard to our time and the contradictions within it.

In particular, with his obstinate refusal of the widespread unconditional surrender to the illogical logic of the world, abandoned to the blind faith in globalization—in such a way as it is called today, in a discrete as well as anodyne way, the "commercial anarchy"—Fichte's reflection keeps on highlighting how the duty for the future is, first of all, to remove the inevitability of the morphology of the existing reality, and in a complementary way, to unmask the ideology of the unchangeability of the actual reality. Secondly, the necessity to prompt the uninterrupted effort aimed at transforming the state of things follows; and this is while being aware that "reality should be judged starting from the ideals and modified by those who feel they are able to."

In the presence of a sociopolitical cosmos that presents itself with the opaque traits of the immutable and, therefore, as a "thing per se," it becomes possible to uphold—by varying Heidegger's formula in a Fichtian register—that only an *I* can save us, by removing the inevitability of the *not-I* and by concretely acting in a social and communitarian way in order to distance it from the logic of the meaninglessness presented as a destiny, like an inevitable as well as untranscendable outcome.

It is in this sense that in these times, according to Novalis' valuable suggestion, we are called to "fichtise better than Fichte" (*besser fichtisiren als Fichte*).[274] This means to take back Fichte's project of rejuvenation of the world through

---

[274] Novalis, *Schriften, a cura di R. Samuel* – H.-J. Mähl – G. Schulz, (Stuttgart: Kolhammer, 1960-2006), 6 voll., II, p. 524. See B. Loheide, *Fichte und Novalis. Transzendentalphilosophisches Denken im romantisierenden Diskurs*, (Amsterdam: Rodopi, 2000).

praxis and thereon, to redialectalize the reality by breaking up the absolutistic mysticism of necessity in which our time is suspended, in which the fatalism of the disenchanted witness makes the morphology of the actuality fatal. In this scenario of completed sinfulness, where cynicism and adaptability paint the dominant emotional shades, Fichte's hearty words, pregnant with expectations, resound as a total opposition to our age. In his *Sun-Clear Statement* (1868), he writes:

> *In the present age, the Doctrine of Knowledge has no other hopes and pretensions that it may not be thrown aside and forgotten altogether, but may pass into at least a few, who can transmit it to a better age.*[275]

Likewise, Hölderlin's vibrant words echo: "[Fichte is] a titan who fights for humanity and whose circle of influence will not remain within the walls of the auditorium."[276]

---

[275] J.G. Fichte, *Sun-Clear Statement*, 1801, Wikisource.
[276] It is in such a way that Hegel, in his letter to Schelling at the end of January 1795, summons Hölderlin's opinion on Fichte's lectures in which he took part. See *Briefe von und an Hegel*, ed by di J. Hoffmeister; Italian translation ed. by P. Manganaro, Epistolario, (Naples: Guida, 1983), ss., I, p. 111. English translation by A. Carnesecchi.